The Statesman's Manual; Or, The Bible The Best Guide To Political Skill And Foresight: A Lay Sermon. [Followed By] A Lay Sermon, Addressed To The Higher And Middle Classes, On The Existing Distresses And Discontents

Samuel Taylor Coleridge

Nabu Public Domain Reprints:

You are holding a reproduction of an original work published before 1923 that is in the public domain in the United States of America, and possibly other countries. You may freely copy and distribute this work as no entity (individual or corporate) has a copyright on the body of the work. This book may contain prior copyright references, and library stamps (as most of these works were scanned from library copies). These have been scanned and retained as part of the historical artifact.

This book may have occasional imperfections such as missing or blurred pages, poor pictures, errant marks, etc. that were either part of the original artifact, or were introduced by the scanning process. We believe this work is culturally important, and despite the imperfections, have elected to bring it back into print as part of our continuing commitment to the preservation of printed works worldwide. We appreciate your understanding of the imperfections in the preservation process, and hope you enjoy this valuable book.

LAY SERMONS;
BY S. T. COLERIDGE, ESQ.

THE STATESMAN'S MANUAL;

OR

THE BIBLE THE BEST GUIDE TO POLITICAL SKILL AND FORESIGHT:

A LAY SERMON,

ADDRESSED TO

THE HIGHER CLASSES OF SOCIETY.

By S. T. COLERIDGE, Esq.

BURLINGTON:
CHAUNCEY GOODRICH.
1832.

University Press.
C., GOODRICH....Printer.

LAY SERMON.

PSALM LXXVIII. V. 5, 6, 7.

5. For he established a testimony in Jacob and appointed a law in Israel; which he commanded our fathers, that they should make them known to their children. 6. That the generation to come might know them, even the children which should be born; who should arise and declare them to their children: 7. That they might set their hope in God, and not forget the works of God.

If our knowledge and information concerning the Bible had been confined to the one fact of its immediate derivation from God, we should still presume that it contained rules and assistances for all conditions of men under all circumstances; and therefore for communities no less than for individuals. The contents of every work must correspond to the character and designs of the work-master; and the inference in the present case is too obvious to be overlooked, too plain to be resisted. It requires, indeed, all the might of superstition to conceal from a man of common understanding the further truth, that the interment of such a treasure in a dead language must needs be contrary to the intentions of the gracious Donor. Apostacy itself dared not question the *premise:* and that the practical *consequence* did not follow, is conceivable only under a complete *system* of delusion, which from the cradle to the deathbed ceases not to overawe the will by obscure fears, while it pre-occupies the senses by vivid imagery and ritual pantomime. But to such a scheme all forms of sophistry are native. The very excellence of the Giver has been made a reason for withholding the gift; nay the transcendent value of the gift itself assigned as the motive of its detention. We may be shocked at the presumption, but need not be surprized at the fact, that a jealous priesthood should have ventured to represent the applicability of the Bible to all the wants and occasions of men as a wax-like pliability to all their fancies and prepossessions. Faithful guardians of Holy Writ! they are constrained to make it useless in order to guard it from profanation; and those, whom they have most defrauded, are the readiest to justify the fraud. For imposture, organized into a comprehensive and self-consistent whole, forms a world of its own, in which inversion becomes the order of nature.

Let it not be forgotten, however, (and I recommend the fact to the especial attention of those among ourselves, who are disposed to rest contented with an implicit faith and passive acquiescence) that the Church of Superstition never ceased to avow the profoundest reverence for the Scriptures themselves, and what it forbids its vassals to ascertain, it not only permits, but commands them to *take for granted*.

Whether, and to what extent, this suspension of the rational functions, this spiritual slumber, will be imputed as a sin to the souls who are still under chains of papal darkness, we are neither enabled or authorized to determine. It is enough for us to know that the land, in which we abide, has like another Goshen *been severed from the plague,* and that we have light in *our* dwellings. The road of salvation for *us* is a high road, and the wayfarers, though 'simple, need not err therein.' The Gospel lies open in the market-place, and on every window seat, so that (*virtually* at least) the deaf may hear the words of the Book! It is preached at every turning, so that the blind may see them. (Isai. xxix. 18.) The circumstances then being so different, if the result should prove similar, we may be quite certain that *we* shall not be held guiltless. The ignorance, which may be the excuse of others, will be our crime. Our birth and denizenship in an enlightened and protestant land, will, with all our rights and franchises to boot, be brought in judgment against us, and stand first in the fearful list of blessings abused. The glories of our country will form the blazonry of our own impeachment, and the very name of Englishmen, which we are almost all of us too proud of, and scarcely any of us enough thankful for, will be annexed to that of Christians only to light up our shame, and aggravate our condemnation.

I repeat, therefore, that the habitual unreflectingness, which in certain countries may be susceptible of more or less palliation in most instances, can in this country be deemed blameless in none. The humblest and least educated of our countrymen must have wilfully neglected the inestimable privileges, secured to all alike, if he has not himself found, if he has not from his own personal experience discovered, the sufficiency of the Scriptures in all knowledge requisite for a right performance of his duty as a man and a christian. Of the laboring classes, who in all countries form the great majority of the inhabitants, more than this is not demanded, more than this is not perhaps generally desirable—"They are not sought for in public counsel, nor need they be found where politic sentences are spoken.——It is enough if every one is wise in the working of his own craft: so best will they maintain the state of the world."

But you, my friends, to whom the following pages are more particularly addressed, as to men moving in the higher class of society:— You will, I hope, have availed yourselves of the ampler means entrusted to you by God's providence, to a more extensive study and a wider use of his revealed will and word. From you we have a right to expect a sober and meditative accommodation to your own times and country of those important truths declared in the inspired writings 'for a thousand generations,' and of the awful examples, belonging to all ages, by which those truths are at once illustrated and confirmed. Would you feel conscious that you had shewn yourselves unequal to your station in society—would you stand degraded in your own eyes; if you betrayed an utter want of information respecting the acts of human sovereigns and legislators? And should you not much rather be both ashamed and afraid to know yourselves inconversant with the acts and constitutions of God whose law executeth itself, and whose Word is the foundation, the power, and the life of the universe? Do you hold it a requisite of your rank to shew yourselves inquisitive concerning the expectations and plans of statesmen and state-counsellors? Do you excuse it as natural curiosity, that you lend a listening ear to the guesses of state-gazers, to the dark hints and open revilings of our self-inspired state fortune-tellers, '*the wizards, that peep and mutter*' and forcast, alarmists by trade, and malecontents for their bread? And should you not feel a deeper interest in predictions which are permanent prophecies, because they are at the same time eternal truths? Predictions which in containing the grounds of fulfilment involve the principles of foresight, and teach the science of the future in its perpetual elements?

But I will struggle to believe that of those whom I now suppose myself addressing, there are few who have not so employed their greater leisure and superior advantages as to render these remarks, if not wholly superfluous, yet personally inapplicable. In commmon with your worldly inferiors, you will indeed have directed your *main* attention to the promises and the information conveyed in the records of the evangelists and apostles: promises, that need only a lively trust in them, on our own part, to be the means as well as the pledges of our *eternal* welfare! information that opens out to our knowledge a kingdom that is not of this world, thrones that cannot be shaken, and sceptres that can neither be broken or transferred! Yet not the less on this account will you have looked back with a proportionate interest on the *temporal* destinies of men and nations, stored up for our instruction in the archives of the Old Testament: not the less will you delight to retrace the paths by which Providence has led the kingdoms of *this* world through the valley of mortal life—Paths, engraved with the foot-marks of captains sent forth from the God of Armies! Nations in whose guidance or chastisement the arm of Omnipotence itself was made bare.

Recent occurrences have given additional strength and fresh force to our sage poet's eulogy on the Jewish prophets:

> As men divinely taught and better teaching
> The solid rules of civil government
> In their majestic unaffected style,
> Than all the oratory of Greece and Rome.
> In them is plainest taught and easiest learnt
> What makes a nation happy and keeps it so,
> What ruins kingdoms and lays cities flat.
> PARADISE REGAINED, iv. 354.

If there be any antidote to that restless craving for the wonders of the day, which in conjunction with the appetite for publicity is spreading like an efflorescence on the surface of our national character; if there exist means for deriving resignation from general discontent, means of building up with the very materials of political gloom that stedfast frame of hope which affords the only certain shelter from the throng of self-realizing alarms, at the same time that it is the natural home and workshop of all the active virtues; that antidote and these means must be sought for in the collation of the present with the past, in the habit of thoughtfully assimilating the events of our own age to those of the time before us. If this be a moral advantage derivable from history in general, rendering its study therefore a moral duty for such as possess the opportunities of books, leisure and education, it would be inconsistent even with the *name* of believers not to recur with pre-eminent interest to events and revolutions, the records of which are as much distinguished from all other history by their especial claims to divine authority, as the facts themselves were from all other facts by especial manifestation of divine interference. 'Whatsoever things,' saith Saint Paul (Romans xv. 4.) 'were written aforetime, were written for our learning; that we through patience and comfort of the Scriptures might have hope.'

In the infancy of the world, signs and wonders were requisite in order to startle and break down that superstition, idolatrous in itself and the source of all other idolatry, which tempts the natural man to seek the true cause and origin of public calamities in outward circumstances, persons and incidents: in agents therefore that were themselves but surges of the same tide, passive conductors of the one invisible influence, under which the total host of billows, in the whole line of successive impulse, swell and roll shoreward; there finally, each in its turn, to strike, roar and be dissipated.

But with each miracle worked there was a truth revealed, which thence forward was to act as its substitute: And if we think the Bible less applicable to us on account of the miracles, we degrade ourselves into mere slaves of sense and fancy, which are indeed the appointed medium between earth and heaven, but for that very cause stand in a desirable relation to spiritual truth then only, when, as a mere and passive medium, they yield a free passage to its light. It was only to overthrow the usurpation exercised in and through the senses, that the senses were miraculously appealed to. Reason and Religion are their own evidence. The natural Sun is in this respect a symbol of the spiritual. Ere he is fully arisen, and while his glories are still under veil, he calls up the breeze to chase away the usurping vapours of the night-season, and thus converts the air itself into the minister of its own purification: not surely in proof or elucidation of the light from heaven, but to prevent its interception.

Wherever, therefore, similar circumstances co-exist with the same moral causes, the principles revealed, and the examples recorded, in the inspired writings render miracles superfluous: and if we neglect to apply truths in expectation of wonders, or under pretext of the cessation of the latter, we tempt God and merit the same reply which our Lord gave to the Pharisees on a like occasion. 'A wicked and an adulterous generation seeketh after a sign, and there shall no sign be given to it, but the sign of the prophet Jonas:' that is, a threatening call to repentance. Equally applicable and prophetic will the following verses be. 'The men of Nineveh shall rise in judgment with this generation and shall condemn it, because they repented at the preaching of Jonas, and behold, a greater than Jonas is here.—The queen of the South shall rise up in the judgment with this generation, and shall condemn it: for she came from the uttermost parts of the earth to hear the wisdom of Solomon, and behold a greater than Solomon is here.' For have we not divine assurance that Christ is with his church, even to the end of the world? And what could the queen of the South, or the men of Nineveh have beheld, that could enter into competition with the events of our own times, in importance, in splendor, or even in strangeness and significancy?

The true origin of human events is so little susceptible of that kind of evidence which can *compel* our belief; so many are the disturbing forces which in every cycle or ellipse of changes modify the motion given by the first projection; and every age has, or imagines it has, its own circumstances which render past experience no longer applicable to the present case; that there will never be wanting answers, and explanations, and specious flatteries of hope to persuade a people and its government, that the history of the past is inapplicable to *their* case. And no wonder, if we read history for the facts instead of reading it for the sake of the general principles, which are to the facts as the root and sap of a tree to its leaves: and no wonder, if history so read should find a dangerous rival in novels, nay, if the latter should be preferred to the former on the score even of probability. I well remember, that when the examples of former Jacobins, as Julius Cæsar, Cromwell, and the like, were adduced in France and England at the commencement of the French Consulate, it was ridiculed as pedantry and pedant's ignorance to fear a repetition of usurpation and military despotism at the close of the ENLIGHTENED EIGHTEENTH CENTURY! Even so, in the very dawn of the late tempestuous day, when the revolutions of Corcyra, the prescriptions of the Reformers, Marius, Cæsar, &c., and the direful effects of the levelling tenets in the Peasant's War in Germany, (differenced from the tenets of the first French constitution only by the mode of wording them, the figures of speech being borrowed in the one instance from theology, and in the other from modern metaphysics) were urged on the Convention, and its vindicators; the magi of the day, the true citizens of the world, the Plusquam-perfecti of patriotism, gave us set proofs that similar results were *impossible*, and that it was an insult to so philosophical an age, to so enlightened a nation, to dare direct the public eye towards them as to lights of warning. Alas! like lights in the stern of a vessel they illuminated the path only that had been passed over!

The politic Florentine* has observed, that there are brains of three races. The one understands of itself; the other understands as much as is shown it by others; the third neither understands of itself, nor what is shewn it by others. In our times there are more perhaps who belong to the third class from vanity and acquired frivolity of mind, than from natural incapacity. It is no uncommon foible with those who are honoured with the acquaintance of the great, to attribute national events to particular persons, particular measures, to the errors of one man, to the intrigues of another, to any possible spark of a particular occasion, rather than to the true proximate cause, (and which alone deserves the name of a cause) the predominant state of public opinion. And still less are they inclined to refer the latter to the ascendancy of speculative principles, and the scheme or mode of thinking in vogue. I have known men, who with significant nods and the pitying contempt of smiles, have denied all influence to the corruptions of moral and political

---

* Sono di tre generazioni cervelli: l'uno intende per se; l'altro intende quanto da altri gli e mostro; il terzo non intende né per se stesso ne per demostrazione d'altri.—MACHIAVELLI.

philosophy, and with much solemnity have proceeded to solve the riddle of the French Revolution by ANECDOTES! Yet it would not be difficult, by an unbroken chain of historic facts, to demonstrate that the most important changes in the commercial relations of the world had their origin in the closets or lonely walks of uninterested theorists;—that the mighty epochs of commerce, that have changed the face of empires; nay, the most important of those discoveries and improvements in the mechanic arts, which have numerically increased our population beyond what the wisest statesmen of Elizabeth's reign deemed possible, and again doubled this population virtually; the most important, I say, of those inventions that in their results

―――――― best uphold
War by her two main nerves, iron and gold;

had their origin not in the cabinets of statesmen, or in the practical insight of men of business, but in the closets of uninterested theorists, in the visions of recluse genius. To the immense majority of men, even in civilized countries, speculative philosophy has ever been and must ever remain, a terra incognita. Yet it is not the less true, that all the *epoch-forming* Revolutions of the Christian world, the revolutions of religion and with them the civil, social, and domestic habits of the nations concerned, have coincided with the rise and fall of metaphysical systems. So few are the minds that really govern the machine of society, and so incomparably more numerous and more important are the indirect consequences of things than their foreseen and direct effects.

It is with nations as with individuals. In tranquil moods and peaceable times we are quite *practical*. Facts only and cool common sense are then in fashion. But let the winds of passion swell, and straightway men begin to generalize; to connect by remotest analogies; to express the most universal positions of reason in the most glowing figures of fancy; in short, to feel particular truths and mere facts, as poor, cold, narrow, and incommensurate with their feelings.

The Apostle of the Gentiles quoted from a Greek comic poet. Let it not then be condemned as unseasonable or out of place, if I remind you that in the intuitive knowledge of this truth, and with his wonted fidelity to nature, our own great poet has placed the greater number of his profoundest maxims and general truths, both political and moral, not in the mouths of men at ease, but of men under the influence of passion, when the mighty thoughts overmaster and become the tyrants of the mind that has brought them forth. In his Lear, Othello, Macbeth, Hamlet, principles of deepest insight and widest interest fly off like sparks from the glowing iron under the loud anvil. It seems a paradox only to the unthinking, and it is a fact that none, but the unread in history, will deny, that in periods of popular tumult and innovation the more abstract a notion is, the more readily has it been found to combine, the closer has appeared its affinity, with the feelings of a people and with all their immediate impulses to action. At the commencement of the French revolution, in the remotest villages every tongue was employed in echoing and enforcing the almost geometrical abstractions of the physiocratic politicians and economists. The public roads were crowded with armed enthusiasts disputing on the inalienable sovereignty of the people, the imprescriptible laws of the pure reason, and the universal constitution, which, as rising out of the nature and rights of man as man, all nations alike were under the obligation of adopting. Turn over the fugitive writings, that are still extant, of the age of Luther; peruse the pamphlets and loose sheets that came out in flights during the reign of Charles the First and the Republic; and you will find in these one continued comment on the aphorism of Lord Chancellor Bacon (a man assuredly sufficiently acquainted with the extent of secret and personal influence) that the knowledge of the speculative principles of men in general between the age of twenty and thirty, is the one great source of political prophecy. And Sir Philip Sidney regarded the adoption of one set of principles in the Netherlands, as a proof of the divine agency and the fountain of all the events and successes of that revolution.

A calm and detailed examination of the facts justifies me to my own mind in hazarding the bold assertion, that the fearful blunders of the late dread revolution, and all the calamitous mistakes of its opponents from its commencement even to the æra of loftier principles and wiser measures (an æra, that began with, and ought to be named from, the war of the Spanish and Portuguese insurgents) every failure with all its gloomy results may be unanswerably deduced from the neglect of some maxim or other that had been established by clear reasoning and plain facts in the writings of Thucydides, Tacitus, Machiavel, Bacon, or Harrington. These are red-letter names even in the almanacks of worldly wisdom; and yet I dare challenge all the critical benches of infidelity to point out any one important truth, any one efficient, practical direction or warning, which did not pre-exist, and for the most part in a sounder, more intelligible, and more comprehensive form in the Bible.

In addition to this, the Hebrew legislator, and the other inspired poets, prophets, historians and moralists of the Jewish church have two immense advantages in their favour. First, their particular rules and prescripts flow directly and visibly from universal principles, as from a fountain: they flow from principles and ideas that are not so properly said to be confirmed by reason as to be reason itself! Principles, in act and procession, disjoined from which, and from the emotions that inevitably accompany the actual intuition of their truth, the widest maxims of prudence are like arms without hearts, muscles without nerves. Secondly, from the very nature of these principles, as taught in the Bible, they are understood in exact proportion as they are believed and felt. The regulator is never separated from the main spring. For the words of the apostle are literally and philosophically true: WE (that is, the human race) LIVE BY FAITH. Whatever we do or know, that in kind is different from the brute creation, has its origin in a determination of the reason to have faith and trust in itself. This, its first act of faith is scarcely less than identical with its own being. *Implicite*, it is the COPULA—it contains the *possibility*—of every position, to which there exists any correspondence in reality. It is itself, therefore, the realizing principle, the spiritual substratum of the whole complex body of truths. This primal act of faith is enunciated in the word, GOD: a faith not derived from experience, but its ground and source, and without which the fleeting *chaos of facts* would no more form experience, than the dust of the grave can of itself make a living man. The imperative and oracular form of the inspired Scripture is the form of reason itself in all things purely rational and moral.

If it be the word of Divine Wisdom, we might anticipate that it would in all things be distinguished from other books, as the Supreme Reason, whose knowledge is creative, and antecedent to the things known, is distinguished from the understanding, or creaturely mind of the individual, the acts of which are posterior to the things, it records and arranges. Man alone was created in the image of God: a position groundless and inexplicable, if the reason in man do not differ from the understanding. For this the inferior animals, (many at least) possess *in degree:* and assuredly the divine image or idea is not a thing of degrees.

Hence it follows that what is *expressed* in the inspired writings, is *implied* in all absolute science. The latter whispers what the former utter as with the voice of a trumpet. As SURE AS GOD LIVETH, is the pledge and assurance of every positive truth, that is asserted by the reason. The human understanding *musing on* many things, snatches at truth, but is frustrated and disheartened by the fluctuating nature of its objects; * its conclusions therefore are timid and uncertain, and it hath no way of giving permanence to things but by reducing them to abstractions: hardly (saith the author of the Wisdom of Solomon, of whose words the preceding sentence is a paraphrase) hardly do we guess aright at things that are upon earth, and with labour do we find the things that are before us; but all certain knowledge is in the power of God, and a presence from above. So only have the ways of men been reformed, and every doctrine that contains a *saving* truth, and all acts pleasing to God (in other words, all actions consonant with human nature, in its original intention) are through WISDOM: that is, the *rational* spirit of man.

This then is the prerogative of the Bible; this is the privilege of its believing students.

---

* Ποταμῷ γὰρ οὐκ ἔςι δὶς ἐμβῆναι τῷ αὐτῷ καθ' Ἡράκλειτον, οὔτε θνητῆς οὐσίας δὶς ἅψασθαι κατὰ ἕξιν· ἀλλὰ ὀξύτητι καὶ τάχει τῆς μεταβολῆς σκίδνησι καὶ πάλιν συνάγει, μᾶλλον δὲ οὐδὲ πάλιν οὐδὲ ὕςερον ἀλλ' ἅμα συνίςαται καὶ ἀπολείπει, καὶ πρόσεισι καὶ ἄπεισι· ὅθεν οὐδ' εἰς τὸ εἶναι περαίνει τὸ γιγνόμενον αὐτῆς τῷ μηδέποτε λήγειν μηδ' ἥττασθαι τὴν γένεσιν.

PLUTARCH, *Edit. Hutt. cap.* XVIII. *Vol. p.* IX. 239.

With them the principle of knowledge is likewise a spring and principle of action. And as it is the only *certain* knowledge, so are the actions that flow with it the only ones on which a secure reliance can be placed. The understanding may suggest motives, may avail itself of motives, and make judicious conjectures respecting the probable consequences of actions. But the knowledge taught in the Scriptures *produces* the motives, *involves* the consequences; and its highest formula is still: As sure as God liveth, so will it be unto thee! Strange as this position will appear to such as forget that motives can be causes only in a secondary and improper sense, inasmuch as the man makes the motive, not the motives the man; and that the same thought shall be a motive to one man and no motive to his neighbour; (a sufficient proof that the motives themselves are effects, the principle of which, good or evil, lies far deeper)—matter for scorn and insult though this position will furnish to those, who think (or try to think) every man *out of his senses* who has not lost his reason (or alienated it by wilful sophistry, demanding reasons for reason itself) yet all history bears evidence to its truth. The sense of expediency, the cautious balancing of comparative advantages, the constant wakefulness to the Cui bono?—in connection with the Quid mihi?—all these are in their places in the routine of conduct, by which the individual provides for himself the real or supposed wants of to-day and to-morrow: and in quiet times and prosperous circumstances a nation presents an aggregate of such individuals, a busy ant-hill in calm and sunshine. By the happy organization of a well-governed society the contradictory interests of ten millions of such individuals may neutralize each other, and be reconciled in the unity of the rational interest. But whence did this happy organization first come?—Was it a tree transplanted from Paradise, with all its branches in full fruitage?—Or was it sowed in sunshine?—Was it in vernal breezes and gentle rains that it fixed its roots, and grew and strengthened?—Let History answer these questions!—With blood was it planted—it was rocked in tempests—the goat, the ass, and the stag gnawed it—the wild boar has whetted his tusk on its bark. The deep scars are still extant on its trunk, and the path of the lightning may be traced among its higher branches. And even after its full growth, in the season of its strength, 'when its height reached to the heaven, and the sight thereof to all the earth,' the whirlwind has more than once forced its stately top to touch the ground: it has been bent like a bow, and sprang back like a shaft. Mightier powers were at work than Expediency ever yet called up!—yea, mightier than the mere Understanding can comprehend! One confirmation of the latter assertion you may find in the history of our country, written by the same Scotch philosopher, who devoted his life to the undermining of the Christian religion; and expended his last breath in a blasphemous regret that he had not survived it!—by the same heartless sophist who, in this island, was the main pioneer of that atheistic philosophy, which in France transvenomed the natural thirst of truth into the hydrophobia of a wild and homeless scepticism; the Elias of that Spirit of Antichrist, which

> ———— still promising
> Freedom, itself too sensual to be free,
> Poisons life's amities and cheats the soul
> Of faith, and quiet hope and all that lifts
> And all that soothes the spirit!

*3

This inadequacy of the mere understanding to the apprehension of moral greatness we may trace in this historian's cool systematic attempt to steal away every feeling of reverence for every great name by a scheme of *motives*, in which as often as possible the efforts and enterprizes of heroic spirits are attributed to this or that paltry view of the most despicable selfishness. But in the majority of instances this would have been too palpably false and slanderous; and therefore the founders and martyrs of our church and constitution, of our civil and religious liberty, are represented as fanatics and bewildered enthusiasts. But histories incomparably more authentic than Mr. Hume's, (nay, spite of himself even his own history) confirm by irrefragable evidence the aphorism of ancient wisdom, that nothing great was ever achieved without enthusiasm. For what is enthusiasm but the oblivion and swallowing-up of self in an object dearer than self, or in an idea more vivid?—How this is produced in the enthusiasm of wickedness, I have explained in the third Comment annexed to this Discourse. But in the genuine enthusiasm of morals, religion, and patriotism, this enlargement and elevation of the soul above its mere self attest the presence, and accompany the intuition of ultimate PRINCIPLES alone. These alone can interest the undegraded human spirit deeply and enduringly, because these alone belong to its essence, and will remain with it permanently.

Notions, the depthless abstractions of fleeting phenomena, the shadows of sailing vapors, the colorless repetitions of rain-bows, have effected their utmost when they have added to the *distinctness* of our knowledge. For this very cause they are of themselves adverse to lofty emotion, and it requires the influence of a light and warmth, not their own, to make them chrystallize into a semblance of growth. But every principle is actualized by an idea; and every idea is living, productive, partaketh of infinity, and (as Bacon has sublimely observed) containeth an endless power of semination. Hence it is, that science, which consists wholly in ideas and principles, is power. Scientia et potentia (saith the same philosopher) in idem coincident. Hence too it is, that notions, linked arguments, reference to particular facts and calculations of prudence, influence only the comparatively few, the men of leisurely minds who have been trained up to them: and even these few they influence but faintly. But for the reverse, I appeal to the general character of the doctrines which have collected the most numerous sects, and acted upon the moral being of the converts with a force that might well seem supernatural! The great PRINCIPLES of our religion, the sublime IDEAS spoken out everywhere in the Old and New Testament, resemble the fixed stars, which appear of the same size to the naked as to the armed eye; the magnitude of which the telescope may rather seem to diminish than to increase. At the annunciation of *principles*, of *ideas*, the soul of man awakes, and starts up, as an exile in a far distant land at the unexpected sounds of his native language, when after long years of absence, and almost of oblivion, he is suddenly addressed in his own mother-tongue. He weeps for joy, and embraces the speaker as his brother. How else can we explain the fact so honourable to Great Britain, that the poorest* amongst us will contend with as much enthusiasm as the richest for the rights of property? These rights are the spheres and necessary conditions of free agency. But free agency contains the idea of the free will; and in this he intuitively knows the sublimity, and the infinite hopes, fears, and capabilities of his own nature. On what other ground but the cognateness of ideas and principles to man as man, does the nameless soldier rush to the combat in defence of the liberties or the honour of his country?—Even men wofully neglectful of the precepts of religion will shed their blood for its truth.

Alas!—the main hindrance to the use of the Scriptures, as your Manual, lies in the notion that you are already acquainted with its contents. Something *new* must be presented to you, wholly new and wholly out of yourselves; for whatever is within us must be as old as the first dawn of human reason. Truths of all

---

* The reader will remember the anecdote told with so much humour in Goldsmith's Essay. But this is not the first instance where the mind in its hour of meditation finds matter of admiration and elevating thought, in circumstances that in a different mood had excited its mirth.

others the most awful and mysterious and at the same time of universal interest, are considered as so true as to lose all the powers of truth, and lie bed-ridden in the dormitory of the soul, side by side, with the most despised and exploded errors. But it should not be so with you! The pride of education, the sense of consistency should preclude the objection: for would you not be ashamed to apply it to the works of Tacitus, or of Shakespeare? Above all, the rank which you hold, the influence you possess, the powers you may be called to wield, give a special unfitness to this frivolous craving for novelty. To find no contradiction in the union of the old and new, to contemplate the ANCIENT OF DAYS, his words and his works, with a feeling as fresh as if they were now first springing forth at his fiat—this characterizes the minds that feel the riddle of the world and may help to unravel it! This, most of all things, will raise you above the mass of mankind, and therefore will best entitle and qualify you to guide and controul them! You say, you are already familiar with the Scriptures. With the *words*, perhaps, but in any other sense you might as wisely boast of your familiar acquaintance with the rays of the sun, and under that pretence turn away your eyes from the light of Heaven.

Or would you wish for authorities?—for great examples?—You may find them in the writings of Thuanus, of Lord Clarendon, of Sir Thomas More, of Raleigh; and in the life and letters of the heroic Gustavus Adolphus. But these, though eminent statesmen were christians, and might lie under the thraldom of habit and prejudice. I will refer you then to authorities of two great men, both pagans; but removed from each other by many centuries, and not more distant in their ages than in their characters and situations. The first shall be that of Heraclitus, the sad and recluse philosopher. Πολυμαθίη νοον ο'ν διδάσκει· Σίβυλλα δὲ μαινομένῳ ςοματι 'αγέλαςα και α'καλλωπιςα καί 'αμύριςα φθεγγομένη χιλίων ετῶν ἐξικνεῖται τῇ φωνῇ δια τὸν θεόν.* Shall we hesitate to apply to the prophets of God, what could be affirmed of the Sibylls by a philosopher whom

---

* TRANSLATION.—Multiscience (or a variety and quantity of acquired knowledge) does not teach intelligence. But the SIBYLL with wild enthusiastic mouth shrilling forth unmirthful, inornate, and unperfumed truths reaches to a thousand years with her voice through the power of God.

Socrates, the prince of the philosophers, venerated for the profundity of his wisdom?

For the other, I will refer you to the darling of the polished court of Augustus, to the man whose works have been in all ages deemed the models of good sense, and are still the pocket companions of those who pride themselves on uniting the scholar with the gentleman. This accomplished man of the world has given an account of the subjects of conversation between the illustrious statesmen who governed, and the brightest luminaries who then adorned, the empire of the civilized world:

>Sermo oritur non de villis domibusve alienis
>Nec, male, nec ne lepus saltet. Sed quod magis ad nos
>Pertinet, et nescire malum est, agitamus: utrumne
>Divitiis homines, an sint virtute beati?
>Et quo sit natura boni? summumque quid eius?*
>   Horat. Sermon, L. II. Sat. 6. v. 71.

---

* TRANSLATION.—Conversation arises not concerning the country seats or families of strangers in a neighbourhood, or whether the dancing hare performed well or ill. But we discuss what more nearly concerns us, and which it is an evil not to know: whether men are made happy by wealth or by virtue? In what consists the nature of good? And what is the Supreme good and to be our ultimate aim?

Berkeley indeed asserts, and is supported in his assertion by the great statesmen, Lord Bacon and Sir Walter Raleigh, that without an habitual interest in these subjects a man may be a dexterous intriguer, but never can be a statesman. (The FRIEND No. 5.)

But do you require some one or more particular passage from the Bible, that may at once illustrate and exemplify its applicability to the changes and fortunes of empires? Of the numerous chapters that relate to the Jewish tribes, their enemies and allies, before and after their division into two kingdoms, it would be more difficult to state a single one, from which some guiding light might *not* be struck. And in nothing is Scriptural history more strongly contrasted with the histories of highest note in the present age, than in its freedom from the hollowness of abstractions. While the latter present a shadow-fight of Things and Quantities, the former gives us the history of Men, and balances the important influence of individual Minds with the previous state of the national morals and manners, in which, as constituting a specific susceptibility, it presents to us the true cause both of the Influence itself, and of the Weal or Woe that were its consequents. How should it be otherwise? The histories and political economy of the present and preceding century partake in the general contagion of its mechanic philosophy, and are the *product* of an unenlivened generalizing Understanding. In the Scriptures they are the living *educts* of the Imagination; of that reconciling and mediatory power, which incorporating the Reason in Images of the Sense, and organizing (as it were) the flux of the Senses by the permanence and self-circling energies of the Reason, gives birth to a system of symbols, harmonious in themselves, and consubstantial with the truths, of which they are the *conductors*. These are the Wheels which Ezekiel beheld, when the hand of the Lord was upon him, and he saw visions of God as he sate among the captives by the river of Chebar. *Whithersoever the Spirit was to go, the wheels went, and thither was their spirit to go: for the spirit of the living creature was in the wheels also.* The truths and the symbols that represent them move in conjunction and form the living chariot that bears up (for *us*) the throne of the Divine Humanity. Hence, by a derivative, indeed, but not a divided, influence, and though in a secondary yet in more than a metaphorical sense, the Sacred Book is worthily intitled *the* WORD OF GOD. Hence too, its contents present to us the stream of time continuous as Life and a symbol of Eternity, inasmuch as the Past and the Future are virtually contained in the Present. According therefore to our relative position on its banks the Sacred History becomes prophetic, the Sacred Prophecies historical, while the power and substance of both inhere in its Laws, its Promises, and its Comminations. In the Scriptures therefore both Facts and Persons must of necessity have a two-fold significance, a past and a future, a temporary and a perpetual, a particular and a universal application. They must be at once Portraits and Ideals.

Eheu! paupertina philosophia in paupertinam religionem ducit:—A hunger-bitten and idealess philosophy naturally produces a starveling and comfortless religion. It is among the miseries of the present age that it recognizes no medium between *Literal* and *Metaphorical.* Faith is either to be buried in the dead letter, or its name and honours usurped by a counterfeit product of the mechanical understanding, which in the blindness of self-complacency confounds SYMBOLS with ALLEGORIES. Now an Allegory is but a translation of abstract notions into a picture-language which is itself nothing but an abstraction from objects of the senses; the principal being more worthless even than its phantom proxy, both alike unsubstantial, and the former shapeless to boot. On the other hand a Symbol (ὅ ἔϛιν ἀεὶ ταυτηγόρικον) is characterized by a translucence of the Special in the Individual or of the General in the Especial or of the Universal in the General. Above all by the translucence of the Eternal through and in the Temporal. It always partakes of the Reality which it renders intelligible; and while it enunciates the whole, abides itself as a living part in that Unity, of which it is the representative. The other are but empty echoes which the fancy arbitrarily associates with apparitions of matter, less beautiful but not less shadowy than the sloping orchard or hill-side pasture-field seen in the transparent lake below. Alas! for the flocks that are to be led forth to such pastures! *It shall even be as when the hungry dreameth, and behold! he eateth; but he waketh and his soul is empty: or as when the thirsty dreameth, and behold he drinketh; but he awaketh and is faint!"* (Isaiah xxix. 8.) O! that we would seek for the bread which was given from heaven, that we should eat thereof and be strengthened! O that we would draw at the well at which the flocks of our fore-fathers had living water drawn for them, even that water which, instead of mocking the thirst of him to whom it is given, becomes a well within himself springing up to life everlasting!

When we reflect how large a part of our present knowledge and civilization is owing, directly or indirectly, to the Bible; when we are compelled to admit, as a fact of history, that the Bible has been the main Lever by which the moral and intellectual character of Europe has been raised to its present comparative height; we should be struck, me thinks, by the marked and prominent difference of this Book from the works which it is now the fashion to quote as guides and authorities in morals, politics and history. I will point out a few of the excellencies by which the one is distinguished, and shall leave it to your own judgment and recollection to perceive and apply the contrast to the productions of highest name in these latter days. In the Bible every agent appears and acts as a self-subsisting individual: each has a life of its own, and yet all are one life. The elements of necessity and free-will are reconciled in the higher power of an omnipresent Providence, that predestinates the whole in the moral freedom of the integral parts. Of this the Bible never suffers us to lose sight. The root is never detached from the ground. It is God everywhere: and all creatures conform to his decrees, the righteous by performance of the law, the disobedient by the sufferance of the penalty.

Suffer me to inform or remind you, that there is a threefold Necessity. There is a logical, and there is a mathematical, necessity; but the latter is always hypothetical, and both subsist *formally* only, not in any real object. Only by the intuition and immediate spiritual consciousness of the idea of God, as the One and Absolute, at once the Ground and the Cause, who alone containeth in himself the ground of his own nature, and therein of *all* natures, do we arrive at the third, which alone is a real *objective,* necessity. Here the immediate consciousness decides: the idea is its own evidence, and is insusceptible of all other. It is necessarily groundless and indemonstrable; because it is itself the ground of all possible demonstration. The Reason hath faith in itself, in its own revelation. Ο ΛΟΓΟΣ ΕΦΗ. IPSE DIXIT! So it is: for it is so! All the necessity of causal relations (which the mere understanding reduces, and must reduce to co-existence and regular succession* in the objects of which they are predicated, and to habit and association in the mind predicating) depends on, or rather inheres in, the idea of the Omnipresent and Absolute: for this it is, in which the Possible is one and the same with the Real and the Necessary. Herein the Bible differs from all the books of Greek philosophy, and in a two-fold manner. It doth not affirm a Divine Nature only, but a God: and not a God only, but the living God. Hence in the Scriptures alone is the *Jus divinum*, or direct Relation of the State and its Magistracy to the Supreme Being, taught as a vital and

---

* See Hume's Essays. The sophist evades, as Cicero long ago remarked, the better half of the predicament, which is not "præire" but "*efficienter* præire."

indispensable part of all moral and of all political wisdom, even as the Jewish alone was a true theocracy.

But I refer to the demand. Were it my object to touch on the present state of public affairs in this kingdom, or on the prospective measures in agitation respecting our sister-island, I would direct your most serious meditations to the latter period of the reign of Solomon, and to the revolutions in the reign of Rehoboam, his successor. But I should tread on glowing embers. I will turn to a subject on which all men of reflection are at length in agreement—the causes of the revolution and fearful chastisement of France. We have learned to trace them back to the rising importance of the commercial and manufacturing class, and its incompatibility with the old feudal privileges and prescriptions; to the spirit of sensuality and ostentation, which from the court had spread through all the towns and cities of the empire; to the predominance of a presumptuous and irreligious philosophy; to the extreme over-rating of the knowledge and power given by the improvements of the arts and sciences, especially those of astronomy, mechanics, and a wonder-working chemistry; to an assumption of prophetic power, and the general conceit that states and governments might be and ought to be constructed as machines, every movement of which might be foreseen and taken into previous calculation; to the consequent multitude of plans and constitutions, of planners and constitution-makers, and the remorseless arrogance with which the authors and proselytes of every new proposal were ready to realize it, be the cost what it might in the established rights, or even in the lives, of men; in short, to restlessness, presumption, sensual indulgence, and the idolatrous reliance on false philosophy in the whole domestic, social, and political life of the stirring and effective part of the community: these all acting, at once and together, on a mass of materials supplied by the unfeeling extravagance and oppressions of the government, which 'shewed no mercy, and very heavily laid its yoke.'

Turn then to the chapter from which the last words were cited, and read the following seven verses; and I am deceived if you will not be compelled to admit, that the Prophet

Isaiah revealed the true philosophy of the French revolution more than two thousand years before it became a sad irrevocable truth of history. 'And thou saidst, I shall be a lady for ever: so that thou didst not lay these things to thy heart, neither didst remember the latter end of it. Therefore, hear now this, thou that art given to pleasures, that dwellest carelessly, that sayest in thine heart, I am, and none else besides me! I shall not sit as a widow, neither shall I know the loss of children. But these two things shall come to thee in a moment, in one day; the loss of children, and widowhood; they shall come upon thee in their perfection, for the multitude of thy sorceries, and for the abundance of thine enchantments. For thou hast trusted in thy wickedness; thou hast said, there is no overseer. Thy wisdom and thy knowledge, it hath perverted thee; and thou hast said in thine heart, I am, and none else besides me. Therefore shall evil come upon thee, thou shalt not know*

---

* The reader will scarcely fail to find in this verse a remembrancer of the sudden setting-in of the frost, a fortnight before the usual time (in a country too, where the commencement of its two seasons is in general scarcely less regular than

from whence it riseth: and mischief shall fall upon thee, thou shalt not be able to put it off; and desolation shall come upon thee suddenly, which thou shalt not know. Stand now with thine enchantments, and with the multitude of thy sorceries, wherein thou hast laboured from thy youth; if so be thou shalt be able to profit, if so be thou mayest prevail. Thou art wearied in the multitude of thy counsels: let now the astrologers, the stargazers, the monthly prognosticators stand up, and save thee from these things that shall come upon thee.'

There is a grace that would enable us to take up vipers, and the evil thing shall not hurt us: a spiritual alchemy which can transmute poisons into a panacæa. We are counselled by our Lord himself to make unto ourselves friends of the mammon of Unrighteousness: and in

---

that of the wet and dry seasons between the tropics) which caused, and the desolation which accompanied, the flight from Moscow. The Rusians baffled the *physical* forces of the imperial Jacobin, because they were inaccessible to his *imaginary* forces. The faith in St. Nicholas kept off at safe distance the more pernicious superstition of the Destinies of Napoleon the Great. The English in the Peninsula overcame the real, because they *set at defiance*, and had heard only to despise, the imaginary powers of the irresistible Emperor. Thank heaven, the heart of the country was sound at the *core*.

this age of sharp contrasts and grotesque combinations it would be a wise method of sympathizing with the tone and spirit of the Times, if we elevated even our daily news-papers and political journals into COMMENTS ON THE BIBLE.

When I named this Essay a Sermon, I sought to prepare the inquirers after it for the absence of all the usual softenings suggested by worldly prudence of all compromise between truth and courtesy. But not even as a Sermon would I have addressed the present Discourse to a promiscuous audience; and for this reason I likewise announced it in the title-page, as exclusively *ad clerum;* i. e. (in the old and wide sense of the word) to men of *clerkly* acquirements, of whatever profession. I would that the greater part of our publications could be thus *directed,* each to its appropriate class of Readers. But this cannot be! For among other odd burs and kecksies, the misgrowth of our luxuriant activity, we have now a READING PUBLIC*—as strange a phrase, methinks,

---

* Some particle passive in the diminutive form ERUDITOLORUM NATIO for instance, might seem at first sight a fuller and more exact designation; but the superior force and hu-

as ever forced a splenetic smile on the staid countenance of Meditation; and yet no fiction! For our Readers have, in good truth, multiplied exceedingly, and have waxed proud. It would require the intrepid accuracy of a Colquhoun to venture at the precise number of

mor of the former become evident whenever the phrase occurs as a step or stair in a *climax* of irony. By way of example take the following sentences, transcribed from a work *demonstrating* that the New Testament was intended exclusively for the primitive converts from Judaism, was accommodated to their prejudices, and is of no authority, as a rule of faith, for Christians in general. 'The READING PUBLIC in this ENLIGHTENED AGE, and THINKING NATION, by its favourable reception of LIBERAL IDEAS, has long demonstrated the benign influence of that PROFOUND PHILOSOPHY which has already emancipated us from so many absurd prejudices held in superstitious awe by our deluded forefathers. But the *Dark Age* yielded at length to the dawning light of Reason and Common-Sense at the glorious, though imperfect, Revolution. THE PEOPLE can be no longer duped or scared out of their *imprescriptible and inalienable* RIGHT to judge and decide for themselves on all important questions of Government and Religion. The *scholastic jargon* of jarring articles and metaphysical creeds may continue for a time to deform our Church-establishment; and like the grotesque figures in the nitches of our old gothic cathedrals may serve to remind the nation of its former barbarism; but the *universal suffrage* of a FREE AND ENLIGHTENED PUBLIC," &c. &c.!

Among the Revolutions worthy of notice, the change in the nature of the introductory sentences and prefatory matter in that vast company only, whose heads and hearts are dieted at the two public *ordinaries* of Literature, the circulating libraries and the periodical press. But what is the result? Does the inward man thrive on this regimen? Alas! if the average health of the consumers may be judged of by the articles of largest consumption; if the secretions may be conjectured from the ingredients of the dishes that are found best suited to their palates; from all that I have seen, either of the banquet or the guests, I

serious Books is not the least striking. The same gross flattery which disgusts us in the dedications to individuals in the elder writers, is now transferred to the Nation at large or the READING PUBLIC: while the Jeremiads of our old Moralists, and their angry denunciations concerning the ignorance, immorality, and irreligion of the *People*, appear (mutatis mutandis, and with an appeal to the worst passions, envy, discontent, scorn, vindictiveness, &c.) in the shape of bitter libels on Ministers, Parliament, the Clergy: in short, on the State and Church, and all persons employed in them. Likewise, I would point out to the Reader's attention the marvellous predominance at present of the *words*, Idea and Demonstration. Every talker now a days has an *Idea*; aye, and he will demonstrate it too! A few days ago, I heard one of the READING PUBLIC, a thinking and independent smuggler, *euphonize* the latter word with much significance, in a tirade against the planners of the late African expedition:—" *As to Algiers, any man that has half an* IDEA *in his skull, must know, that it has been long ago dey-monstered, I should say,* dey-mon-

shall utter my *Profaccia* with a desponding sigh. From a popular philosophy and a philosophic populace, Good Sense deliver us!

At present, however, I am to imagine for myself a very different audience. I appeal exclusively to men, from whose station and opportunities I may dare anticipate a respectable portion of that "*sound book learnedness*," into which our old public schools still continue to initiate their pupils. I appeal to men in whom I may hope to find, if not philosophy, yet occasional impulses at least to philosophic thought. And here, as far as my own experience extends, I can announce one favourable

---

strified, &c." But the phrase, which occasioned this note, brings to my mind the mistake of a lethargic Dutch traveller, who returning highly gratified from a showman's caravan, which he had been tempted to enter by the words, THE LEARNED PIG, gilt on the pannels, met another caravan of a similar shape, with THE READING FLY on it, in letters of the same size and splendour. "Why, dis is voonders above voonders!" exclaims the Dutchman, takes his seat as first comer, and soon fatigued by waiting, and by the very hush and intensity of his expectation, gives way to his constitutional somnulence, from which he is roused by the supposed showman at Hounslow, with a "*In what name, Sir! was your place taken? Are you booked all the way for Reading?*—Now a Reading Public is (to my mind) more marvellous still, and in the third tier of " voonders above voonders."

symptom. The notion of our measureless superiority in good sense to our ancestors, so general at the commencement of the French Revolution, and for some years before it, is out of fashion. We hear, at least, less of the jargon of this *enlightened age*. After fatiguing itself, as performer or spectator in the giddy figure-dance of political changes, Europe has seen the shallow foundations of its self-complacent faith give way; and among men of influence and property, we have now more reason to apprehend the stupor of despondence, than the extravagancies of hope, unsustained by experience, or of self-confidence not bottomed on principle.

In this rank of life the danger lies, not in any tendency to innovation, but in the choice of the means for preventing it. And here my apprehensions point to two opposite errors; each of which deserves a separate notice. The first consists in a disposition to think, that as the Peace of Nations has been disturbed by the diffusion of a false light, it may be re-established by excluding the people from all knowledge and all prospect of amelioration. O! never, never! Reflection and stirrings of mind, with all their restlessness, and all the errors that result from their imperfection, from the *Too much*, because *Too little*, are come into the world. The Powers, that awaken and foster the spirit of curiosity, are to be found in every village: Books are in every hovel. The infant's cries are hushed with *picture-books*: and the Cottager's child sheds his first bitter tears over pages, which render it impossible for the man to be treated or governed as a child. Here as in so many other cases, the inconveniences that have arisen from a things' having become too general, are best removed by making it universal.

The other and contrary mistake proceeds from the assumption, that a national education will have been realized whenever the People at large have been taught to read and write. Now among the many means to the desired end, this is doubtless one, and not the least important. But neither is it the most so. Much less can it be held to *constitute* Education, which consists in *educing* the faculties, and forming the habits; the means varying according to the sphere in which the individuals to be educated are likely to act and become useful. I do not hesitate to declare, that whether I consider the nature of the discipline adopted,* or the plan of poisoning the children of the poor with a sort of *potential* infidelity under the "*liberal idea*" of teaching those points only of religious faith, in which all denominations agree, I cannot but denounce the so called Lancastrian schools as pernicious beyond all power of compensation by the new acquirement of Reading and Writing.—But take even Dr. Bell's original and unsophisticated plan, which I myself regard as an especial gift of Providence to the *human race;* and suppose this incomparable machine, this vast moral steam-engine to have been adopted and in free motion throughout the Empire; it would yet appear to me a most dangerous delusion to rely on it as if this of itself formed an efficient national education. We cannot, I repeat, honour

---

* See Mr. Southey's Tract on the New or Madras system of Education: especially toward the conclusion, where with exquisite humour as well as with his usual poignancy of wit he has detailed Joseph Lancaster's disciplinarian Inventions. But even in the schools, that used to be called Lancastrian, these are, I believe, discontinued. The true perfection of discipline in a school is—The maximum of watchfulness with the minimum of punishment.

the scheme too highly as a prominent and necessary part of the great process; but it will neither supersede nor can it be substituted for sundry other measures, that are at least equally important. And these are such measures too, as unfortunately involve the necessity of sacrifices on the side of the rich and powerful more costly, and far more difficult than the yearly subscription of a few pounds! such measures as demand more self-denial than the expenditure of time in a committee or of eloquence in a public meeting.

Nay, let Dr. Bell's philanthropic end have been realized, and the proposed medicum of learning universal: yet convinced of its insufficiency to stem up against the strong currents *set in* from an opposite point, I dare not assure myself, that it may not be driven backward by them and become confluent with the evils, it was intended to preclude.

What other measures I had in contemplation, it has been my endeavour to explain elsewhere. But I am greatly deceived, if one preliminary to an efficient education of the labouring classes be not the recurrence to a more manly discipline of the intellect on the part of the learned themselves, in short a thorough recasting of the moulds, in which the minds of our Gentry, the characters of our future Landowners, Magistrates and Senators, are to receive their shape and fashion. O what treasures of practical wisdom would be once more brought into open day by the solution of this problem! Suffice it for the present to hint the masterthought. *The first man, on whom the Light of an* IDEA *dawned, did in that same moment receive the spirit and the credentials of a Lawgiver:* and as long as man shall exist, so long will the possession of that antecedent knowledge (the maker and master of all profitable Experience) which exists only in the power of an *Idea,* be the one lawful qualification of all Dominion in the world of the senses. Without this, Experience itself is but a cyclops walking backwards, under the fascination of the Past: and we are indebted to a lucky coincidence of outward circumstances and contingencies, least of all things to be calculated on in times like the present, if this one-eyed Experience does not seduce its worshipper into practical anachronisms.

But alas! the halls of old philosophy have

been so long deserted, that we circle them at shy distance as the haunt of Phantoms and Chimæras. The sacred Grove of Academus is held in like regard with the unfoodful trees in the shadowy world of Maro that had a dream attached to every leaf. The very terms of ancient wisdom are worn out, or (far worse!) stamped on baser metal: and whoever should have the hardihood to reproclaim its solemn Truths must commence with a Glossary.

In reviewing the foregoing pages, I am apprehensive that they may be thought to resemble the overflow of an earnest mind rather than an orderly premeditated composition. Yet this imperfection of form will not be altogether uncompensated, if it should be the means of presenting with greater liveliness the feelings and impressions under which they were written. Still less shall I regret this defect if it should induce some future traveller engaged in the like journey to take the same station and to look through the same medium at the one main object which amid all my discursions I have still held in view. The more, however, doth it behoove me not to conclude this address without attempting to recapitulate in as few and as plain words as possible the sum and substance of its contents.

There is a state of mind indispensable for all perusal of the Scriptures to edification, which must be learnt by experience, and can be described only by negatives. It is the direct opposite of that which (supposing a *moral* passage of Scripture to have been cited) would prompt a man to reply, *Who does not know this?* But if the quotation should have been made in support of some article of *faith*, this same habit of mind will betray itself, in different individuals, by apparent contraries, which yet are but the two poles, or *Plus* and *Minus* states, of the same influence. The latter, or the *negative* pole may be suspected, as often as you hear a comment on some high and doctrinal text introduced with the words, *It only means so and so!* For instance, I object to a professed *free-thinking* christian the following solemn enunciation of "*the riches of the glory of the mystery hid from ages and from generations*" by the philosophic Apostle of the Gentiles. "*Who* (viz. the Father) *hath delivered us from the power of darkness and hath translated us into the kingdom of his dear Son: In* *whom we have redemption through his blood, even the forgiveness of sins: Who is the image of the invisible God, the first born* of every creature: For by him were all things created, that are in heaven, and that are in earth, visible and invisible, whether they be thrones, or dominions, or principalities, or powers: all things were created by him, and for him: And he is before all things, and by him all things consist. And he is the head of the body, the Church: who is the beginning, the first born from the dead; that in all things he might have the preeminence. For it pleased the Father that in him should all fulness dwell: And, having made peace through the blood of his cross, by him to reconcile all things unto himself; by him, I say whether they be things in earth, or things in heaven."* What is the reply?—Why, that by these words (very bold and figurative words it must be confessed, yet still) St. Paul *only* meant that the universal and eternal truths of morality and a future state had been reproclaimed by an

---

* A mistaken translation. The words should be: Begotten before all creation; and even this does not convey the *full* sense of the superlative, πρωτοτοκος. The present version makes the following words absurd.

inspired teacher and confirmed by miracles! The words *only* mean, Sir, that a state of retribution after this life had been proved by the fact of Christ's resurrection—that is all!—But I shall scarcely obtain an answer to certain difficulties involved in this free and liberal interpretation: ex. gr. that with the exception of a handful of rich men considered as little better than infidels, the Jews were as fully persuaded of these truths as Christians in general are at the present day. Moreover that this inspired Teacher had himself declared that if the Jews did not believe on the evidence of Moses and the Prophets, neither would they though a man should rise from the dead.

Of the positive pole, on the other hand, language to the following purport is the usual Exponent. "It is a mystery: and we are bound to believe the words without presuming to enquire into the meaning of them."• That is we believe in St. Paul's *veracity;* and that is enough. Yet St. Paul repeatedly presses on his Hearers that thoughtful perusal of the Sacred Writings, and those habits of earnest though humble enquiry which if the heart only have been previously re-generated would lead them "to a full *assurance* of Understanding εἰς ἐπίγνωσιν, (*to an entire assent of the mind; to a spiritual intuition, or positive inward knowledge by experience*) of the Mystery of God, *and* of the Father, and of Christ, in which (nempe, μυστηρίῳ) are hid all the treasures of wisdom and knowledge.

To expose the inconsistency of both these extremes, and by inference to recommend that state of mind, which looks forward to "*the fellowship of the mystery of the faith as a spirit of wisdom and revelation in the* KNOWLEDGE *of God, the eyes of the* UNDERSTANDING *being* enlightened—this formed my GENERAL purpose. Long has it been at my heart! I consider it as the contra-distinguishing principle of Christianity that in it alone πᾶς πλᾶτος τῆς πληροφορίας τῆς Συνέσεως (the Understanding in its utmost power and opulence) *culminates* in Faith, as in its crown of Glory, at once its light and its remuneration. On this most important point I attempted long ago to preclude, if possible, all misconception and misinterpretation of my opinions, though in a work which, from the mode of its publication and other circumstances must be unknown or known but by *name* to the great majority of my present Readers. Alas! in this time of distress and embarrassment the sentiments have a more especial interest, a more immediate application, than when they were first written. If (I observed) it be a Truth attested alike by common feeling and common sense, that the greater part of human Misery depends directly on human Vices, and the remainder indirectly, by what means can we act on Men, so as to remove or preclude these Vices and purify their principles of moral election? The question is not by what means each man is to alter his own character—in order to this, all the means prescribed, and all the aidances given by religion may be necessary for him. Vain of themselves may be—

> The sayings of the Wise
> In ancient and in modern books enroll'd
> . . . .
> Unless he feel within
> Some source of consolation from above,
> Secret refreshings, that repair his strength,
> And fainting spirits uphold.
>
> SAMPSON AGONISTES.

This is not the question. Virtue would not be Virtue could it be *given* by one fellow creature to another. To *make use* of all the means and appliances in our power to the actual attainment of Rectitude, is the abstract of the Duty which we owe to ourselves: To *supply* those means as far as we can, comprizes our Duty to others. The question then is, what are these means? Can they be any other than the communication of Knowledge and the removal of those Evils and Impediments which prevent it's reception? It may not be in our power to combine both, but it is in the power of every man to contribute to the former, who is sufficiently informed to feel that it is his Duty. If it be said, that we should endeavour not so much to remove Ignorance, as to make the Ignorant religious: Religion herself, through her sacred oracles, answers for me, that all effective Faith pre-supposes Knowledge and individual Conviction. If the mere acquiescence in Truth, uncomprehended and unfathomed, were sufficient, few indeed would be the vicious and the miserable, in this country at least where speculative Infidelity is, Heaven be praised, confined to a small number. Like bodily deformity, there is one instance here and another there; but three in one place are already an undue proportion. It is highly worthy of observation, that the inspired Writings received by Christians are distinguishable from all other books pretending to Inspiration, from the scriptures of the Bramins, and even from the Koran, in their strong and frequent recommendations of Truth. I do not here mean Veracity, which cannot but be enforced in every Code which appeals to the religious principle of Man; but Knowledge. This is not only extolled as the Crown and Honor of a Man, but to seek after it is again and again commanded us as one of our most sacred Duties. Yea, the very perfection and final bliss of the glorified spirit is represented by the Apostle as a plain aspect, or intuitive beholding of truth in it's eternal and immutable source. Not that Knowledge can of itself do all! The light of religion is not that of the moon, light without heat; but neither is it's warmth that of the stove, warmth without light. Religion is the sun whose warmth indeed swells, and stirs, and actuates the life of nature, but who at the same time beholds all the growth of life with a master-eye, makes all objects glorious on which he looks, and by that glory visible to others. For this cause I bow my knees unto the Father of our Lord Jesus Christ, that he would grant you according to the riches of his glory, to be strengthened with might by his Spirit in the inner man; that Christ may dwell in your hearts by faith; that ye being rooted and grounded in love, may be able to comprehend with all saints what is the breadth, and length, and depth and heighth; and to know the love of Christ which passeth all knowledge, that ye might be filled with the fulness of God. For to know God is (by a vital and spiritual act in which to know and to possess are one and indivisible) to acknowledge him as the Infinite Clearness in the Incomprehensible Fulness, and Fulness Incomprehensible with Infinite Clearness.

This then comprizes my first purpose, which is in a two fold sense *general:* for in the *substance*, if not in the form, it belongs to all my countrymen and fellow-christians without distinction of Class, while for its object it embraces the whole of the inspired Scriptures from the recorded first day of Heaven and Earth, ere the light was yet gathered into celestial lamps or reflected from their revolving mirrors, to the predicted Sabbath of the New Creation, when Heaven and Earth shall have become one city with neither "sun nor moon to shine in it: for the glory of God shall lighten it and the Lamb be the light thereof." My second purpose is after the same manner in a two fold sense *specific*: for as this Disquisition is nominally addressed to, so was it for the greater part exclusively intended for, the perusal of THE LEARNED: and its object likewise is to urge men so qualified to apply their powers and attainments to an especial study of the Old Testament as teaching the Elements of Political Science.

Is it asked, in what sense I use these words? I answer: in the same sense as the terms are employed when we refer to Euclid for the Elements of the Science of Geometry, only with one difference arising from the diversity of the subject. With one difference only; but that one how momentous! All other sciences are confined to abstractions, unless when the term Science is used in an improper and flattering sense—Thus we may speak without boasting of NATURAL HISTORY; but we have not yet attained to a SCIENCE of Nature. The

Bible alone contains a Science of *Realities:* and therefore each of it's Elements is at the same time a living GERM, in which the Present involves the Future, and in the Finite the Infinite exists potentially. That hidden mystery in every, the minutest, form of existence, which contemplated under the relations of time presents itself to the understanding retrospectively, as an infinite ascent of Causes, and prospectively as an interminable progression of Effects—that. which contemplated in Space is beheld intuitively as a law of action and re-action, continuous and extending beyond all bound—this same mystery freed from the phenomena of Time and Space, and seen in the depth of *real* Being, reveals itself to the pure Reason as the actual immanence of ALL in EACH. Are we struck with admiration at beholding the Cope of Heaven imaged in a Dew-drop? The least of the animalcula to which that drop would be an Ocean contains in itself an infinite problem of which God Omni-present is the only solution. The slave of custom is roused by the Rare and the Accidental alone; but the axioms of the Unthinking are to the philosopher the deepest problems as being the nearest to the mysterious ROOT and partaking at once of its darkness and its pregnancy.

O what a mine of undiscovered treasures, what a new world of Power and Truth would the Bible promise to our future meditation, if in some gracious moment one solitary text of all its inspired contents should but dawn upon us in the pure untroubled brightness of an IDEA, that most glorious birth of the God-like within us, which even as the Light, its material symbol, reflects itself from a thousand surfaces, and flies homeward to its Parent Mind enriched with a thousand forms, itself above form and still remaining in its own simplicity and identity! O for a flash of that same Light, in which the first position of geometric science that ever loosed itself from the generalizations of a groping and insecure experience, did for the first time reveal itself to a human intellect in all its evidence and all its fruitfulness, Transparence without Vacuum, and Plenitude without Opacity! O that a single gleam of our own inward experience would make comprehensible to us the rapturous EUREKA, and the grateful Hecatomb, of the philosopher of Samos! or, that Vision which from the contemplation of an arithmetical harmony rose to the eye of KEPLER, presenting the planetary world, and all their orbits in the Divine order of their ranks and distances: or which, in the falling of an Apple, revealed to the etherial intuition of our own Newton the constructive principle of the material Universe. The promises which I have ventured to hold forth concerning the hidden treasures of the Law and the Prophets will neither be condemned as a paradox or as exaggeration, by the mind that has learnt to understand the possibility, that the reduction of the sands of the Sea to number should be found a less stupendous problem by Archimedes than the simple conception of the Parmenidean ONE. What however is achievable by the human understanding without this light may be comprised in the epithet, κενοσπεδοι: and a melancholy comment on that phrase would the history of human cabinets and Legislatures for the last thirty years furnish! The excellent Barrow, the last of the disciples of Plato and Archimedes among our modern mathematicians, shall give the description and state the value: and in his words I shall conclude.

Aliud agere, to be impertinently busy, doing that which conduceth to no good purpose is in some respect worse than to do nothing. Of such industry we may understand that of the Preacher, "The labor of the foolish wearieth every one of them."

NOTE.—The Appendix to the Statesman's Manual may be found in CHAUNCEY GOODRICH's edition of Coleridge's Aids to Reflection, published in one volume, octavo, in 1829, and edited by DOCTOR MARSH.

A

LAY SERMON,

ADDRESSED TO THE

HIGHER AND MIDDLE CLASSES,

ON THE EXISTING

Distresses and Discontents.

By S. T. COLERIDGE, Esq.

BURLINGTON:
CHAUNCEY GOODRICH.
1832.

INTRODUCTION.

Fellow-Countrymen! You I mean, who fill the higher and middle stations of society! The comforts, perchance the splendors, that surround you, designate your rank, but cannot constitute your moral and personal fitness for it. Be it enough for others to know, that you are its *legal*—but by what mark shall you stand accredited to your own consciences, as its *worthy*—possessors? Not by common sense or common honesty; for these are equally demanded of all classes, and therefore mere negative qualifications in *your* rank of life, or characteristic only by the aggravated ignominy consequent on their absence. Not by genius or splendid talent: for these, as being gifts of Nature, are objects of moral interest for those alone, to whom they have been allotted. Nor yet by eminence in learning; for this supposes such a devotion of time and thought, as would in many cases be incompatible with the claims of active life. Erudition is, doubtless, an *ornament*, that especially becomes a high station: but it is *professional* rank only that renders its attainment a duty.

The mark in question must be so far *common*, that we may be entitled to look for it in *you* from the mere circumstance of your situation, and so far distinctive, that it must be such as cannot be expected generally from the inferior classes. Now either there is no such criterion in existence, or the Desideratum is to be found in *an habitual consciousness of the ultimate principles, to which your opinions are traceable*. The least, that can be demanded of the least favored among you, is an earnest *endeavor* to walk in the Light of your own knowledge; and not, as the *mass* of mankind, by laying hold on the skirts of Custom. Blind followers of a blind and capricious guide, forced likewise (though oftener, I fear, by their own improvidence,* than by the lowness of their estate)

---

* A truth, that should not however be said, save in the spirit of charity, and with the palliating reflection, that this very improvidence has hitherto been, though not the *inevitable*, yet the *natural* result of Poverty and the Poor Laws. With what gratitude I venerate my country and its laws, my humble publications from the "FEARS IN SOLITUDE" printed in 1798, to the present discourse bear witness.—Yet the POOR LAWS and the REVENUE!—if I permitted myself to dwell on these exclusively, I should be tempted to fancy that the domestic seals were put in commission and entrusted to Argus, Briareus, and Cacus, as lords of the commonalty. Alas! it is easy to see the evil; but to imagine a remedy is difficult in exact proportion to the experience and good sense of the seeker. That excellent man, Mr. Perceval, whom I

to consume Life in the means of living, the multitude may make the sad confession

<blockquote>Tempora mutantur: nos et mutamur in illis</blockquote>

unabashed. But to English Protestants in the enjoyment of a present competency, much more to such as are defended against the anxious Future, it must needs be a grievous dishonor, (and not the less grievous, though perhaps less striking, from its frequency) to change with the times, and thus

regard as the best and wisest statesman, this country has possessed since the revolution (I judge only from his measures and the reports of his speeches in parliament: for I never saw him, that I know of) went into the ministry, with the design as well as the wish of abolishing lotteries. I was present at a table, when this intention was announced by a venerable relative of the departed statesman, who loved and honored the *man*, but widely dissented from him as a politician. Except myself, all present were partizans of the opposition; but all avowed their determination on this score alone, as a great moral precedent, to support the new minister.—What was the result? Two lotteries in the first year instead of one! The door of the cabinet has a quality the most opposite to the Ivory Gate of Virgil. It suffers no dreams to pass through it. Alas! as far as any *wide* scheme of benevolence is concerned, the inscription over it might seem to be the Dantèan

<blockquote>Lasciate ogni speranza, voi ch'entrate!</blockquote>

We judge harshly because we expect irrationally. But on the other hand, this disproportion of the power to the wish will, sooner or later, end in that tame acquiescence in things as they are, which is the sad symptom of a moral *necrosis*

to debase their motives and maxims, the sacred house-hold of conscience, into slaves and creatures of fashion. *Thou therefore art inexcusable*, O man! (Rom. II. i.) if thou dost not give to thyself *a reason for the faith that is in thee:* if thou dost not thereby learn the safety and the blessedness of that other apostolic precept *Whatsoever ye do, do it in* Faith. Your habits of reflection should at least be equal to your opportunities of leisure: and to that which is itself a *species* of leisure—your immunity from bodily labor, from the voice and lash of the imperious ever-recurring This Day! Your attention to the objects, that stretch away below you in the living landscape of good and evil, and your researches into their existing or practicable bearings on each other, should be proportional to the elevation that extends and diversifies your prospect. If you possess more than is necessary for your own wants, more than your own wants ought to be felt by you as your own interests. You are pacing on a smooth terrace, which

commencing. And commence it will, if its causes are not counteracted by the philosophy of history, that is, by history read in the spirit of prophecy; if they are not overcome by the faith which, still re-kindling hope, still re-enlivens charity. Without the knowledge of Man, the knowledge of Men is a hazardous acquisition. What insight might not our statesmen acquire from the study of the Bible merely as history, if only they had been previously accustomed to study history in the same spirit, as that in which good men read the Bible!

you owe to the happy institutions of your country,—a terrace on the mountain's breast. To what purpose, by what *moral* right, if you continue to gaze only on the sod beneath your feet? Or if converting means into ends and with all your thoughts and efforts absorbed in selfish schemes of climbing cloudward, you turn your back on the wide landscape, and stoop the lower, the higher you ascend.

The remedial and prospective advantages, that may be rationally anticipated from the habit of contemplating particulars in their universal laws; its tendency at once to fix and to liberalize the morality of private life, at once to produce and enlighten the spirit of public zeal; and let me add, its especial utility in recalling the origin and primary purport of the term, GENEROSITY,* to the heart and thoughts of a populace tampered with by sophists and incendiaries of the revolutionary school; these advantages I have felt it my duty and have made it my main object to press on your serious attention during the whole period of my literary labors from earliest manhood to the present

---

* A genera: the qualities either supposed natural and instinctive to men of noble race, or such as their rank is calculated to inspire, as disinterestedness, devotion to the service of their friends, clients, &c. frankness, &c.

hour.* Whatever may have been the specific theme of my communications, and whether they related to criticism, politics, or religion, still PRINCIPLES, their subordination, their connection, and their application, in all the divisions of our tastes, duties, rules of conduct and schemes of belief, have constituted my chapter of contents.

It is an unsafe partition, that divides opinions without principle from unprincipled opinions. If the latter are not followed by correspondent actions, we are indebted for the escape, not to the agent himself, but to his habits of education, to the sympathies of superior rank, to the necessity of

* In testimony of the fact and no less of the small change, my own public and political principles have undergone, I might appeal to the CONCIONES AD POPULUM, delivered at Bristol in the year 1794; but that, though a few copies were printed, they can scarcely be said to have been published. The first of these "Lay-sermons," (which was likewise the firstling of my authorship) I intend to include in the republication or rather the *rinfaciamento* of the FRIEND. I prefer the latter word, because every part will be omitted which could not be brought to conclusion and completion within the extent allotted to the work (three volumes of the size of the British Essayists;) their place supplied by new articles; and the whole arranged anew. The FRIEND likewise has never been *published* in the ordinary sense of the term. The numbers printed weekly on stamped paper were sent by the post to a scanty number of subscribers and (a sad but important distinction!) to a still scantier number of *subscriptionists.*—φωνᾶντα συνε'τοισιν· ἐς δὲ τὸ Πᾶν ἑρμηνέως χατίζει.

character, often, perhaps, to the absence of temptation from providential circumstances or the accident of a gracious Nature. These, indeed, are truths of all times and places; but I seemed to see especial reason for insisting on them in our own times. A long and attentive observation had convinced me, that formerly MEN WERE WORSE THAN THEIR PRINCIPLES, but that at present the PRINCIPLES ARE WORSE THAN THE MEN.

Few are sufficiently aware how much reason most of us have, even as common moral livers, to thank God for being ENGLISHMEN. It would furnish grounds both for humility towards Providence and for increased attachment to our country, if each individual could but see and feel, how large a part of his innocence he owes to his birth, breeding, and residence in Great Britain. The administration of the laws; the almost continual preaching of moral prudence; the number and respectability of our sects; the pressure of our ranks on each other, with the consequent reserve and watchfulness of demeanor in the superior ranks, and the emulation in the subordinate; the vast depth, expansion and systematic movements of our trade; and the consequent inter-dependence, the arterial or nerve-like *net-work* of property, which make every deviation from outward integrity a calculable loss to the offending individual himself from its mere effects, as obstruction and irregularity; and lastly, the naturalness of doing as others do:—these and the like influences, peculiar, some in the kind and all in the degree, to this privileged island, are the buttresses, on which our foundationless well-doing is upheld, even as a house of cards, the architecture of our infancy, in which each is supported by all.

Well then may we pray, give us peace in our time, O Lord! Well for us, if no revolution, or other general visitation, betray the *true* state of our national morality! But above all, well will it be for us if *even now* we dare disclose the secret to our own souls! Well will it be for as many of us as have duly reflected on the Prophet's assurance, *that we must take root downwards if we would bear fruit upwards;* if we would bear fruit, and *continue* to bear fruit, when the foodful plants that stand straight, only because they grow in company; or whose slender surface-roots owe their whole steadfastness to their intertanglement; have been beaten down by the continued rains, or whirled aloft by the sudden hurricane! Nor have we far to seek for whatever it is most important that we should find. The wisdom from above has not ceased for us! "*The principles of the oracles of God*" (Heb. v. 12.) are still uttered from before the altar! ORACLES, Which we may consult without cost! Before an ALTAR, where no sacrifice is required, but of the vices which unman us! no victims demanded, but the unclean and animal passions, which we may have suffered to house within us, forgetful of our baptismal dedication— no victim, but the spiritual sloth, or goat, or fox, or hog, which lay waste the vineyard that the Lord had fenced and planted for himself.

I have endeavored in a previous discourse to persuade the more highly gifted and educated part of my friends and fellow-christians, that as the *New* Testament sets forth the means and conditions of spiritual convalescence, with all the laws of conscience relative to our future state and permanent Being, so does the *Bible* present to us the elements of *public* prudence, instructing us in the true causes, the surest preventatives, and the only cure, of public evils. The authorities of Raleigh, Clarendon and--Milton must at least exempt me from the blame of singularity, if undeterred by the contradictory charges of paradoxy from one party and of adherence to vulgar and old-fashioned prejudices from the other, I persist in avowing my conviction, that the inspired poets, historians and sententiaries of the Jews, are the clearest teachers of political economy: in short, that their writings* are the STATESMAN'S BEST MANUAL, not only as containing the first principles

* To which I should be tempted with the late Edmund Burke to annex that treasure of prudential wisdom, the Ecclesiasticus. I not only yield, however, to the authority of our Church, but, reverence the judgment of its founders in

and ultimate grounds of state-policy whether in prosperous times or in those of danger and distress, but as supplying likewise the details of their *application*, and as being a full and spacious repository of precedents and facts in proof.

Well therefore (again and again I repeat to you,) well will it be for us if we have provided ourselves from this armory while " yet the day of trouble and of treading down and of perplexity" appears at far distance and only " in the valley of

separating this work from the list of the Canonical Books, and in refusing to apply it to the establishment of any *doctrine*, while they caused it to be "read for example of life and instruction of manners." Excellent, nay, invaluable, as this book is in the place assigned to it by our Church, that place is justified on the clearest grounds. For not to say that the compiler himself, candidly cautions us against the imperfections of his translation, and its *no small* difference from the original Hebrew, as it was written by his grandfather, he so expresses himself in his prologue as to exclude all claims to inspiration or divine authority in any other or higher sense than every writer is entitled to make, who having qualified himself by the careful study of the books of other men had been drawn on to write something himself. But of still greater weight, *practically*, are the objections derived from certain passages of the Book, which savour too plainly of the fancies and prejudices of a jew of Jerusalem: ex. gr. the 25th and 26th verses of chapter L; and of greater still the objections drawn from other passages, as from chapter 41st. which by implication and obvious inference are nearly tautamount to a denial of a future state, and bear too great a resemblance to the ethics of the Greek poets and orators in the substitution of posthumous fame for a *true* resurrection, and a consequent

Vision:" if we have humbled ourselves and have confessed our thin and unsound state, even while "from the uttermost parts of the earth we were hearing songs of praise and glory to the upright nation." (Is. xxii. 5. xxiv. 16.)

But if indeed the day of treading down is present, it is still in our power to convert it into a time of substantial discipline for ourselves, and of enduring benefit to the present generation and to posterity. The splendor of our exploits, during the late war, is less honorable to us than the magnanimity of our views, and our generous confidence in the victory

---

personal endurance; the substitution in short, of a nominal for a real immortality, and lastly from the *prudential* spirit of the maxims in general, in which prudence is taught too much on its own grounds instead of being recommended as the organ or vehicle of a spiritual principle in its existing worldly relations. In short, prudence ceases to be wisdom when it is not to the filial fear of God, and to the sense of the excellence of the divine laws, what the body is to the soul! Now, in the work of the son of Sirach, prudence is both body and soul.

It were perhaps to be wished, that this work, and the wisdom of Solomon had alone received the honor of being accompaniments to the inspired writings, and that these should, with a short precautionary preface and a few notes have been printed in *all* our Bibles. The remaining books might without any loss have been left for the learned or for as many as were prompted by curiosity to purchase them, in a separate volume. Even of the Maccabees not above a third part can be said to possess any historic value, as authentic accounts.

of the better cause. Accordingly, we have obtained a good name, so that the nations around us have displayed a disposition to follow our example and imitate our institutions—too often I fear even in parts where from the difference of our relative circumstances the imitation had little chance of proving more than mimickry. But it will be far more glorious, and to our neighbors incomparably more instructive, if in distresses to which all countries are liable we bestir ourselves in remedial and preventive arrangements which all nations may more or less adopt; inasmuch as they are grounded on principles intelligible to all rational and obligatory on all moral beings; inasmuch as, having been taught by God's word, exampled by God's providence, commanded by God's law, and recommended by promises of God's grace, they alone can form the foundations of a christian community. Do we love our country? These are the principles, by which the true friend of the people is contradistinguished from the factious demagogue. They are at once the rock and the quarry. On these alone and with these alone is the solid welfare of a people to be built. Do we love our own souls? These are the principles, the neglect of which writes hypocrite and suicide on the brow of the professing christian. For these are the keystone of that arch on which alone we can cross the torrent of life and death with safety on the passage;

with peace in the retrospect; and with hope shining upon us from through the cloud, toward which we are travelling. Not, my christian friends! by all the lamps of worldly wisdom clustered in one blaze, can we guide our paths so securely as by fixing our eyes on this inevitable cloud, through which all must pass, which at every step becomes darker and more threatening to the children of this world, but to the children of faith and obedience still thins away as they approach, to melt at length and dissolve into the glorious light, from which as so many gleams and reflections of the same falling on us during our mortal pilgrimage, we derive all principles of true and lively knowledge, alike in science and in morals, alike in communities and in individuals.

It has been my purpose throughout the following discourse to guard myself and my Readers from extremes of all kinds: I will therefore conclude this Introduction by inforcing the maxim in its relation to our religious opinions, out of which, with or without our consciousness, all our other opinions flow, as from their Spring-head and perpetual Feeder. And that I might neglect no innocent mode of attracting or relieving the Reader's attention, I have moulded my reflections into the following

ALLEGORIC VISION.

A felling of sadness, a peculiar melancholy, is wont to take possession of me alike in Spring and in Autumn. But in Spring it is the melancholy of Hope: in Autumn it is the melancholy of Resignation. As I was journeying on foot through the Appennine, I fell in with a pilgrim in whom the Spring and the Autumn and the Melancholy of both seemed to have combined. In his discourse there were the freshness and the colors of April:

> Qual ramicel a ramo,
> Tal da pensier pensiero
> In lui germogliava.

But as I gazed on his whole form and figure, I bethought me of the not unlovely decays, both of age and of the late season, in the stately elm; after the clusters have been plucked from its entwining vines, and the vines are as bands of dried withes around its trunk and branches. Even so there was a memory on his smooth and ample forehead, which blended with the dedication of his steady eyes, that still looked—I know not, whether upward, or far onward, or rather to the line of meeting where the sky rests upon the distance. But how may I express—the breathed tarnish, shall I name it?—on the lustre of the pilgrim's eyes? Yet had it not a sort of strange accordance with their slow and reluctant movement, whenever he turned them to any object on the right hand or on the left? It seemed, methought, as if there lay upon the brightness a shadowy presence of disappointments now unfelt, but never forgotten. It was at once the melancholy of hope and of resignation.

We had not long been fellow-travellers, ere a sudden tempest of wind and rain forced us to seek protection in the vaulted door-way of a lone chapelry: and we sate face to face each on the stone bench along-side the low, wether-stained wall, and as close as possible to the mossy door.

After a pause of silence: Even thus, said he, like two strangers that have fled to the same shelter from the same storm, not seldom do Despair and Hope meet for the first time in the porch of Death! All extremes meet, I answered; but your's was a strange and visionary thought. The better then doth it beseem both the place and me, he replied. From a VISIONARY wilt thou hear a VISION? Mark that vivid flash through this torrent of rain! Fire and water. Even here thy adage holds true, and its truth is the moral of my Vision. I entreated him to proceed. Sloping his face toward the arch and yet averting his eye from it, he seemed to seek and prepare his words: till listening to the wind that echoed within the hollow edifice, and to the rain without,

> Which stole on his thoughts with its two-fold sound,
> The clash hard by and the murmur all round,

he gradually sunk away, alike from me and from his own purpose, and amid the gloom of the storm and in the duskiness of that place he sate like an emblem on a rich man's sepulchre, or like an aged mourner on the sodded grave of an only one, who is watching the wained moon and sorroweth not. Starting at length from his brief trance of abstraction, with courtesy and an atoning smile he renewed his discourse, and commenced his parable.

During one of those short furlows from the service of the Body, which the Soul may sometimes obtain even in this, its militant state, I found myself in a vast plain, which I immediately knew to be the VALLEY OF LIFE. It possessed an astonishing diversity of soils: and here was a sunny spot, and there a dark one, forming just such a mixture of sunshine and shade, as we may have observed on the mountains' side in an April day, when the thin broken clouds are scattered over heaven. Almost in the very entrance of the valley stood a large and gloomy pile, into which I seemed constrained to enter. Every part of the building was crowded with tawdry ornaments and fantastic deformity. On every window was pourtrayed, in glaring and inelegant colors, some horrible tale, or preternatural incident, so that not a ray of light could enter, untinged by the medium through which it passed. The body of the building was full of people, some of them dancing, in and out, in unintelligible figures, with strange ceremonies and antic merriment, while others seemed convulsed with horror, or pining in mad melancholy. Intermingled with these, I observed a number of men, clothed in ceremonial robes, who appeared now to marshal the various groups, and to direct their movements; and now with menacing countenances, to drag some reluctant victim to a vast idol, framed of iron bars intercrossed, which formed at the same time an immense cage, and the form of a human Colossus.

I stood for a while lost in wonder, what these things might mean; when lo! one of the Directors came up to me, and with a stern and reproachful look bade me uncover my head; for that the place, into which I had entered, was the temple of the only true Religion, in the holier recesses of which the great Goddess personally resided. Himself too he bade me reverence, as the consecrated Minister of her Rites. Awe-struck by the name of Religion, I bowed before the Priest, and humbly and earnestly intreated him to conduct me into her presence. He assented. Offerings he took from me, with mystic sprinklings of water and with salt he purified, and with strange sufflations he exorcised me; and then led me through many a dark and winding alley, the dew-damps of which chilled my flesh, and the hollow echoes under my feet, mingled methought, with moanings, affrighted me. At length we entered a large hall where not even a single lamp glimmered. It was made half visible by the wan phosphoric rays which proceeded from inscriptions on the walls, in letters of the same pale and sepulchral light. I could read them, methought; but though each one of the words taken separately I seemed to understand, yet when I took them in sentences, they were riddles and incomprehensible. As I stood meditating on these hard sayings, my guide thus addressed me—The fallible becomes infallible, and the infallible remains fallible. Read and believe: these are MYSTERIES!—In the middle of the vast hall the Goddess was placed. Her features, blended with darkness, rose out to my view, terrible, yet vacant. No definite thought, no distinct image was afforded me: all was uneasy and obscure feeling. I prostrated myself before her, and then retired with my guide, soul-withered, and wondering, and dissatisfied.

As I re-entered the body of the temple, I heard a deep buz as of discontent. A few whose eyes were bright, and either piercing or steady, and whose ample foreheads, with the weighty bar, ridge-like, above the eye-brows, bespoke observation following by meditative thought; and a much larger number who were enraged by the severity and insolence of the priests in exacting their offerings; had collected in one tumultuous groupe, and with a confused outcry of " this is the Temple of Superstition!" after much contumely, and turmoil, and cruel maltreatment on all sides, rushed out of the pile: and I, methought, joined them.

We speeded from the Temple with hasty steps, and had now nearly gone round half the valley, when we were addressed by a woman, tall beyond the stature of mortals, and with a something more than human in her countenance and mien, which yet could by mortals be only felt, not conveyed by words or intelligibly distinguished. Deep reflection, animated by ardent feelings, was displayed in them: and hope, without its uncertainty, and a something more than all these, which I understood not; but which yet seemed to blend all these into a divine unity of expression. Her garments were white and matronly, and of the simplest texture. We enquired her name. My name she replied, is Religion.

The more numerous part of our company, affrighted by the very sound, and sore from recent impostures or sorceries, hurried onwards and examined no farther. A few of us, struck by the manifest opposition of her form and manners to those of the living Idol, whom we had so recently abjured, agreed to follow her, though with cautious circumspection. She led us to an eminence in the midst of the valley, from the top of which we could command the whole plain, and observe the relation of the different parts, of each to the other, and of each to the whole, and of all to each. She then gave us an optic glass which assisted without contradicting our natural vision, and enabled us to see far beyond the limits of the Valley of life: though our eye even thus assisted permitted us only to behold a light and a glory, but what we could not descry, save only that it *was*, and that it was most glorious.

And now with the rapid transition of a dream, I had overtaken and rejoined the more numerous party, who had abruptly left us, indignant at the very name of religion. They journied on, goading each other with remembrances of past oppressions, and never looking back, till in the eagerness to recede from the Temple of Superstition they had rounded the whole circle of the valley. And lo! there faced us the mouth of a vast cavern, at the base of a lofty and almost perpendicular rock, the interior side of which, unknown to them, and unsuspected, formed the extreme and backward wall of the Temple. An impatient crowd, we entered the vast and dusky cave, which was the only perforation of the precipice At the mouth of the cave sate two figures; the first, by her dress and gestures, I knew to be SENSUALITY; the second form, from the fierceness of his demeanor, and the brutal scornfulness of his looks, declared himself to be the Monster BLASPHEMY. He uttered big words, and yet ever and anon I observed that he turned pale at his own courage. We entered. Some remained in the opening of the cave, with the one or the other of its guardians. The rest, and I among them, pressed on, till we reached an ample chamber, that seemed the centre of the rock. The climate of the place was unnaturally cold.

In the furthest distance of the chamber sate an old dim-eyed man, poring with a microscope over the Torso of a statue, which had neither basis, nor feet, nor head; but on its breast was carved, NATURE! To this he continually applied his glass, and seemed enraptured with the various inequalities which it rendered visible on the seemingly polished surface of the marble.—Yet evermore was this delight and triumph followed by expressions of hatred, and vehement railing against a Being, who yet, he assured us, had no existence. This mystery suddenly recalled to me what I had read in the Holiest Recess of the temple of *Superstition*. The old man spoke in diverse tongues, and continued to utter other and most strange mysteries. Among the rest he talked much and vehemently concerning an infinite series of causes and effects, which he explained to be—a string of blind men, the last of whom caught hold of the skirt of the one before him, he of the next, and so on till they were all out of sight: and that they all walked infallibly straight, without making one false step, though all were alike blind. Methought I borrowed courage from surprize, and asked him—Who then is at the head to guide them? He looked at me with ineffable contempt, not unmixed with an angry suspicion, and then replied, "No one." The string of blind men went on for ever without any beginning: for although one blind man could not move without stumbling, yet infinite blindness supplied the want of sight. I burst into laughter, which instantly turned to terror—for as he started forward in rage, I caught a glance of him from behind; and lo! I beheld a monster bi-form and Janus-headed, in the hinder face and shape of which I instantly recognized the dread countenance of SUPERSTITION—and in the terror I awoke.

LAY SERMON.

ISAIAH, xxxii. 20.

Blessed are ye that sow beside all waters.

On all occasions the Beginning should look toward the End; and most of all when we offer counsel concerning circumstances of great distress, and of still greater alarm. But such is our business at present, and the common duty of all whose competence justifies the attempt. And therefore, my Christian Friends and Fellow Englishmen, have I *in a day of trouble and of treading down and of perplexity*, taken my Beginning from this animating assurance of an inspired Messenger to *the Devisers of liberal things*, (xxxii. 8.) who confident in hope are fearless in charity. For to enforce the Precept involved in this gladsome annunciation of the Evangelical Herald, to awaken the lively Feeling which it breathes, and to justify the line of conduct which it encourages, are the End to which my present efforts are directed—the ultimate object of the present Address, to which all the other points, therein discussed, are but introductory and preparative.

'Blessed are ye that sow beside all waters.' It is the assurance of a Prophet, and therefore *Surety* itself to all who profess to receive him as such. It is a Command in the form of a Promise, which at once, instructs us in our duty and forecloses every possible objection to its performance. It is at once our Guide and our Pioneer!—a Breeze from Heaven, which at one and the same time determines our path, impels us along it, and removes before-hand, each overhanging cloud that might have conspired with our own dimness to bewilder or to dishearten us. Whatever our own Despondence may whisper, or the reputed Masters of Political Economy may have seemed to demonstrate, neither by the fears and scruples of the one, or by the confident affirmations of the other, dare we be deterred. They must both be false if the Prophet is true. We will still in the power of that faith which can *hope even against hope* continue to sow beside all waters:

for there is a Blessing attached to it by God himself, to whose eye all consequences are present, on whose will all consequences depend.

But I had also an additional motive for the selection of this verse. Easy to be remembered from its briefness, likely to be remembered from its beauty, and with not a single word in it which the malignant ingenuity of Faction could pervert to the excitement of any dark or turbulent feeling, I chose it both as the Text and Title of this Discourse, that it might be brought under the eye of many thousands who will know no more of the Discourse itself than what they read in the advertisements of it in our public papers.

In point of fact it was another passage of Scripture, the words of another Prophet, that originally occasioned this Address, by one of those accidental circumstances, that so often determine the current of our Thoughts. From a company among whom the distresses of the times and the disappointments of the public expectations had been agitated with more warmth than wisdom, I had retired to solitude and silent meditation. A Bible chanced to lie open on the table, my eyes were cast idly on the page for a few seconds, till gradually as a mist clears away, the following words became visible, and at once fixed my attention. 'We looked for peace, but no good came; for a time of health, and behold trouble.'—I turned to the beginning of the chapter: it was the eighth of the prophet Jeremiah, and having read it to the end, I repeated aloud the verses which had become connected in my memory by their pertinency to the conversation, to which I had been so lately attending: namely the 11th, 15th, 20th, and 22d.

They have healed the hurt of the daughter of my people slightly, saying Peace, Peace, when there is no Peace. We looked for Peace, but no good came: for a time of health, and behold, trouble! The harvest is past, the summer is ended: and we are not saved. Is there no balm in Gilead? Is there no Physician? Why then is not the health of the daughter of my people recovered?

These impassioned remonstrances, these heart-probing interrogatories, of the lamenting Prophet, do indeed anticipate a full, and alas! a too faithful statement of the case, to the public consideration of which we have all of late been so often and so urgently invited, and the inward thought of which our very countenances betray, as by a communion of alarm. In the bold painting of Scripture language, *all faces gather blackness*, the Many at the supposed magnitude of the national embarrssment, the Wise at the more certain and far more alarming evil of its moral accompaniments. And they not only contain the state of the case, but suggest the most natural scheme and order of treating it. I avail myself, therefore, of the passage as a part of my text, with the less scruple because it will be found to supply of itself the requisite link of connection. The case itself, the plain fact admitted by men of all parties among us, is, as I have just observed, and as you will yourselves have felt at the first perusal of the words, described by anticipation in the intermediate verses; yet with such historic precision, so plain and so specifically as to render all comment needless, all application superfluous. Peace has come without the advantages expected from Peace, and on the contrary, with many of the severest inconveniences usually attributable to War. 'We looked for peace, but no good came: for a time of health, and behold trouble. The harvest is past, the summer is ended, and we are not saved.' The inference therefore contained in the preceding verse is unavoidable. Where war has produced no repentance, and the cessation of war has brought neither concord or tranquillity, we may safely cry aloud with the Prophet: They have healed the hurt of the daughter of my people slightly, saying peace, peace, when there is no peace.' The whole remaining subject therefore may be comprized in the three questions implied in the last of the verses, recited to you; in three questions, and in the answers to the same. First, who are they who have hitherto prescribed for the case, and are still tampering with it? What are their qualifications? What has been their conduct? Second, What is the true seat and source of the complaint,—the ultimate causes as well as the immediate occasions? And lastly, What are the appropriate medicines? Who and where are the true physicians?

And first then of those who have been ever loud and foremost in their pretensions to a knowledge both of the disease and the remedy. In a preceding part of the same chapter from which I extracted the line prefixed, the Prophet Isaiah enumerates the conditions of a nation's recovery from a state of depression and peril, and among these one condition which he describes in words that may be without any forced or over-refined interpretations unfolded into an answer to the present question. 'A vile person,' he tells us, 'must no more be called liberal, nor the churl be said to be bountiful. For the vile person shall speak villainy, and his heart will work iniquity to practice hypocrisy and to utter error against the Lord; to make empty the soul of the needy, and he will cause the drink of the thirsty to fail. The instruments also of the churl are evil; he deviseth wicked devices to destroy the poor with lying words, even when the needy speaketh aright. BUT THE LIBERAL DEVISETH LIBERAL THINGS, AND BY LIBERAL THINGS SHALL HE STAND.' (Isaiah, xxxii. 5, 6, 7, 8.)

Such are the political empirics mischievous in proportion to their effrontery, and ignorant in proportion to their presumption, the detection and exposure of whose true characters the inspired statesman and patriot represents as indispensable to the re-establishment of the general welfare, while his own portrait of these impostors whom in a former chapter (ix. 15. 16.) he calls *the tail of the Nation*, and in the following verse, *Demagogues that cause the people to err*, affords to the intelligent believer of all ages and countries the means of detecting them, and of undeceiving all whose own malignant passions have not rendered them blind and deaf and brutish. For these noisy and calumnious zealots, whom (with an especial reference indeed to the factious leaders of the populace who under this name exercised a tumultuary despotism in Jerusalem, at once a sign and a cause of its approaching downfall) St. John beheld in the Apocalyptic vision as a compound of Locust and Scorpion, are not of one place or of one season. They are the perennials of history: and though they may disappear for a time, they exist always in the egg, and need only a distempered atmosphere and an accidental ferment to start up into life and activity.

It is worth our while therefore, or rather it is our duty, to examine with a more attentive eye this representative portrait drawn for us by an infallible master, and to distinguish its component parts, each by itself, so that we may combine without confusing them in our memory; till they blend at length into one physiognomic expression, which whenever the counterpart is obtruded on our notice in the sphere of our own experience, may be at once recognized, and enable us to convince ourselves of the identity by a comparison of feature with feature.

The passage commences with a fact, which to the inexperienced might well seem strange and improbable; but which being a truth nevertheless of our own knowledge, is the more striking and characteristic. Worthless persons of little or no estimation for rank, learning, or integrity, not seldom profligates, with whom debauchery has outwrestled rapacity, easy because unprincipled and generous because dishonest, are suddenly cried up as men of enlarged views and liberal sentiments, our only genuine patriots and philanthropists: and churls, that is, men of sullen tempers and surly demeanor; men tyrannical in their families, oppressive and troublesome to their dependents and neighbors, and hard in their private dealings between man and man; men who clench with one hand what they have grasped with the other; these are extolled as public benefactors, the friends, guardians, and advocates of the poor! Here and there indeed we may notice an individual of birth and fortune

(For great estates enlarge not narrow minds)

who has been duped into the ranks of incendiaries and mob-sycophants by an insane restlessness, and the wretched ambition of figuring as the triton of the minows. Or we may find perhaps a professional man of shewy accomplishments but of a vulgar taste, and shallow acquirements, who in part from vanity, and in part as a means of introduction to practice, will seek notoriety by an eloquence well calculated to set the multitude agape, and excite *gratis* to overt-acts of sedition or treason which he may afterwards be fee'd to defend! These however are but exceptions to the general rule. Such as the Prophet has described, such is the *sort* of men; and in point of historic fact it has been from men of this sort, *that profaneness is gone forth into all the land.* (Jeremiah, xxxiii. 15.)

In harmony with the general character of these false prophets, are the particular qualities assigned to them. First, a passion for vauge and violent invective, an habitual and inveterate predilection for the language of hate, and rage and contumely, an ungoverned appetite for abuse and defamation! THE VILE WILL TALK VILLAINY.

But the fetid flower will ripen into the poisonous berry, and the fruits of the hand follow the blossoms of the slanderous lips. HIS HEART WILL WORK INIQUITY. That is, he will plan evil, and do his utmost to carry his plans into execution. The guilt exists already; and there wants nothing but power and opportunity to condense it into crime and overt-act. *He that hateth his brother is a murderer!* says St. John; and of many and various sorts are the brother-haters, in whom this truth may be exemplified. Most appropriately for our purpose, Isaiah has selected the fratricide of sedition, and with the eagle eye and practised touch of an intuitive demonstrator he unfolds the composition of the character, part by part, in the secret history of the agent's wishes, designs and attempts, of his ways, his means, and his ends. The agent himself, the incendiary and his kindling combustibles, had been already sketched by Solomon, with the rapid yet faithful outline of a master in the art: '*The beginning of the words of his mouth is foolishness and the end of his talk mischievous madness,*' Ecclesiastes, x. 13. If in the spirit of Prophecy,* the wise Ruler had been present to our own times, and their procedures; if while he

---

* Solomon has himself informed us, that beyond wealth and conquest, and as of far greater importance to him, in his arduous office of King and Magistrate, he had *sought through knowledge of wisdom to lay hold on folly*: that is, by the study of *Man*, to arrive at a grounded knowledge of *Men*, and through a previous insight into the nature and conditions of Good to acquire by inference a thorough comprehension of the Evil that arises from its deficiency or perversion. And truly in all points of prudence, public and private, we may accommodate to the Royal Preacher his own words (Ecclesiastes, ii. 12.) *What can the man say that cometh after the King? Even that which hath been said already.*

In a preceding page we have interpreted the fifth trumpet in the Apocalypse, of the Zelotæ during the siege of Jerusalem; to the Romans therefore, and their Oriental Allies, we must refer the sounding of the sixth Angel, in this sublime and magnificent drama acted in Heaven, before the whole Host of Heaven, the personal Friend of the Incarnate God attending as the Representative of Human Nature, and in her

sojourned *in the valley of vision* he had actually heard the very harangues of our reigning demagogues to the convened populace; could he have more faithfully characterized either the speakers or the speeches? Whether in spoken or in printed Addresses, whether in periodical Journals or in yet cheaper implements of irritation, the ends are the same, the process is the same, and the same is their general line of conduct. On all occasions, but most of all and with a more blustering malig-

behalf looking and listening with fearful awe to the prophetic symbols of her destiny! But had I dared imitate the major part of the Commentators, and followed the *fatuous fires* of FANCY, that "shrewd sprite" ever busiest when in the service of pre-conceived partialities and antipathies, I might have suffered my judgment to be seduced by the wonderful *(apparent)* aptness of the symbols, (many of them at least) and extended the application of the first eleven verses to the whole chapter, the former as treating of the Demagogues exclusively, the latter as including their infatuated followers likewise. For what other images, concorporated according to the rules of Hieroglyphic Syntax, could form more appropriate and significant exponents of a seditious and riotous multitude, with the mob-orators, their *Heads* or Leaders, than the thousands of pack-horses (*jumenta sarcinaria*) with *heads* resembling those of a roaring wild beast, with smoke, fire and brimstone (that is, empty, unintelligible, incendiary, calumnious, and offensively foul language) issuing from their mouths? 'For their power is in their *Mouths* and in their *Tails*; and they have *Heads*, and by means of them they do hurt.'

nity, whenever any public distress inclines the lower classes to turbulence, and renders them more apt to be alienated from the government of their country—in all places and at every opportunity pleading *to* the Poor and Ignorant, no where and at no time are they found actually pleading *for* them. Nor is this the worst. They even plead against them. Yes! Sycophants to the *crowd*, enemies of the *individuals*, and well-wishers only to the continuance of

---

The authenticity of this canonical Book rests on the firmest grounds, both of outward testimony and internal evidence. But it has been most strangely abused and perverted from the Millenarians of the primitive Church to the religious Politicians of our own times. My own conception of the Book is, that it narrates in the broad and inclusive form of the ancient Prophets (i. e. in the prophetic power of faith and moral insight irradiated by inspiration) the successive struggles and final triumph of Christianity over the Paganism and Judaism of the then Roman Empire, typified in the Fall of Rome, the destruction of the Old and the (symbolical) descent of the New Jerusalem. Nor do I think its interpretation even in detail attended with any insuperable difficulties.

It was once my intention to have translated the Apocalypse, into verse, as a Poem, holding a mid place between the Epic Narrative and the Choral Drama: and to have annexed a Commentary in Prose. An intention long and fondly cherished, but during many years deferred from an unfeigned sense of my deficiency; and now there remains only the hope and the wish, or rather a feeling between both!

their miseries, they plead *against* the poor and afflicted, under the weak and wicked pretence, that we are to do nothing of what we can, because we cannot do all, that we would wish. Or if this sophistry of sloth (*sophisma pigri*) should fail to check the bounty of the rich, there is still the sophistry of slander in reserve to chill the gratitude of the poor. If they cannot dissuade *the liberal from devising liberal things*, they will at least blacken the motives of his beneficence. If they cannot close the hand of the giver, they will at least embitter the gift in the mouth of the receivers. Is it not as if they had said within their hearts; the sacrifice of charity has been offered indeed in despite of us; *but with bitter herbs shall it be eaten!* (Exod. xii. 8.) Imagined wrongs shall make it distasteful. We will infuse vindictive and discontented fancies into minds, already irritable and suspicious from distress: till the fever of the heart shall coat the tongue with gall and spread wormwood on the palate?

However angrily our demagogues may disclaim all intentions of this kind, such has been their procedure, and it is susceptible of no other interpretation. We all know, that the shares must be scanty, where the dividend bears no proportion to the number of the claimants. Yet He, who satisfied the multitude in the wilderness with a few loaves and fishes, is still present to his church. Small as the portions are, if they are both given and taken in the spirit of his commands, a Blessing will go with each; and *the handful of meal shall not fail, until the day when the Lord bringeth back plenty on the land.* But no Blessing can enter where Envy and Hatred are already in possession; and small good will the poor man have of the food prepared for him by his more favored Brother, if he have been previously taught to regard it as a mess of pottage given to defraud him of his Birth-right.

If then to promise medicine and to administer poison; if to flatter in order to deprave; if to affect love to all and show pity to none; if to exaggerate and misderive the distress of the laboring classes in order to make them turbulent, and to discourage every plan for their relief in order to keep them so; if to skulk from private infamy in the mask of public spirit, and make the flaming patriot privilege the gamester, swindler or adulterer; if to seek amnesty for a continued violation of the laws of God by an equal pertinacity in outraging the laws of the land; if these characterize the hypocrite, we need not look far back or far round for faces, wherein to recognize the third striking feature of this prophetic portrait! When therefore the verifying facts press upon us in real life; when we hear persons, the tyranny of whose will is the only law in their families, denouncing all law as tyranny in public—persons, whose hatred of power in others is in exact proportion to their love of it for themselves; when we behold men of sunk and irretrievable characters, to whom no man would entrust his wife, his sister, or his purse, have the effrontery to propose that we should entrust to them our religion and our country; when we meet with *Patriots*, who aim at an enlargement of the rights and liberties of the people by inflaming the populace to acts of madness that necessitate fetters—pretended heralds of freedom and actual pioneers of military despotism; we will call to mind the words of the prophet Isaiah, and say to ourselves; this is no new thing under the Sun! We have heard it with our own ears, and it was declared to our fathers, and in the old time before them, that one of the main characteristics of demagogues in all ages is, TO PRACTICE HYPOCRISY.

Such, I assert, has been the general line of conduct pursued by the political Empirics of the day; and your own recent experience will attest the truth of the assertion. It was affirmed likewise at the same time, that as the conduct, such was the *process:* and I will seek no other support of this charge, I need no better test both of the men and their works, than the plain question: is there one good feeling, to which they do—is there a single bad passion, to which they do not appeal? If they are the enemies of liberty in general, inasmuch as they tend to make it appear incompatible with public quiet and personal safety, still more emphatically are they the enemies of the liberty of the PRESS in particular; and therein of all the truths human and divine which a free press is the most efficient and only commensurate means of protecting, extending and perpetuating. The strongest, indeed the only plausible, arguments against the education of the lower classes, are derived from the writings of these incendiaries; and if for our neglect of the light that hath been vouchsafed to us beyond measure, the land should be visited with a spiritual dearth, it will have been in no small degree occasioned by the erroneous and wicked principles which it is the trade of these men to propagate. Well therefore has the Prophet made it the fourth mark of these misleaders of the multitude, not alone TO utter error, but TO UTTER ERROR AGAINST THE LORD, TO MAKE EMPTY THE SOUL OF THE HUNGRY! Alas! it is a hard and mournful thing, that the Press should be constrained to call out for the harsh curb of the law against the Press! for how shall the Law predistinguish the ominous screech owl from the sacred notes of Augury, from the auspicious and friendly birds of Warning? And yet will we avoid this seeming injustice, we throw down all fence and bulwark of public decency and public opinion. Already has political calumny joined hands with private slander, and every principle, every feeling, that binds the citizen to his country, the spirit to its Creator, is in danger of being undermined.—Not by reasoning, for from that there is no danger; but—by the mere habit of hearing them reviled and scoffed at with impunity.

Were we to contemplate the evils of a rank and unweeded Press only in its effects on the manners of a people, and on the general tone of thought and conversation, the greater love we bore to literature, and to all the means and instruments of human improvement, the more anxiously should we wish for some Ithuriel spear that might remove from the ear of the ignorant and half-learned, and expose in their own fiendish shape, those reptiles, *inspiring venom and forging illusions as they list,*

<pre>
            ——— thence raise,
   At least distemper'd discontented thoughts,
   Vain hopes, vain aims, inordinate desires.
</pre>

PARADISE LOST.

I feel, my friends! that even the strong and painful interest which, the peculiar state of the times, and almost the occurrences of the hour create, can scarcely counterbalance the wearisome aversion inspired by the deformity and *palpableness* of the subject itself. As the plan originates in the malignant restlessness of desperate ambition or desperate circumstances, so are its means and engines a *drag-net* of Fraud and delusion. THE INSTRUMENTS AL-

SO OF THE CHURL ARE EVIL, HE DEVISETH WICKED DEVICES WITH LYING WORDS. He employs a compound poison, of which the following are the main ingredients, the proportions varying as the case requires or the wit of the poisoner suggests. It will be enough rapidly to name and number the components, as in a catalogue. 1. Bold, warm, and earnest assertions, it matters not whether supported by facts or no, nay, though they should involve absurdities, and demonstrable impossibilities: ex. gr. that the amount of the sinecure places given by the executive power would suffice to remove all distress from the land. He is a bungler in the trade, and has been an indocile scholar of his dark master, the father of lies, who cannot make an assertion pass for a fact with an ignorant multitude. The natural generosity of the human heart which makes it an effort to doubt; the confidence which apparent courage inspires; and the contagion of animal enthusiasm; will ensure the belief. Even in large assemblies of men highly educated it is too often sufficient to place impressive images in juxta-position: and the constitutive forms of the mind itself aided by the power of habit will supply the rest. For we all *think* by causal connections. 2. Startling particular Facts, which, dissevered from their context, enable a man to *convey* falsehood while he *says* truth. 3. Arguments built on passing events and deriving an undue importance from the feelings of the moment. The mere appeal, however, to the auditors whether the arguments are not such that none but an idiot or an hireling could resist, is an effective substitute for any argument at all. For mobs have no memories. They are in nearly the same state as that of an individual when he makes (what is termed) *a Bull*. The passions, like a fused metal, fill up the wide interstices of thought, and supply the defective links: and thus incompatible assertions are harmonized by the *sensation*, without the *sense*, of connection. 4. The display of the defects without the accompanying advantages, or vice versa. 5. Concealment of the general and ultimate result behind the scenery of local, and particular consequences. 6. Statement of positions that are true only under particular conditions, to men whose ignorance or fury make them forget that these conditions are not present, or lead them to take for granted that they are. 7. Chains of Questions, especially of such questions as the persons best authorized to propose are ever the slowest in proposing; and objections intelligible of themselves, the answers to which require the comprehension of a system. 8. Vague and common-place Satire, stale as the wine in which flies were drowned last summer, seasoned by the sly tale and important anecdote of but yesterday, that came within the speaker's own knowledge! 9. Transitions from the audacious charge, not seldom of as signal impudence " as any thing was ever carted for," to the lie pregnant and interpretative: the former to prove the orator's courage, and that he is neither to be bought or frightened; the latter to flatter the sagacity of the audience.

———— δῆλός ἐ'ϛιν α'υτόθεν
Ἐν πανουργίᾳ τε καὶ θράσει καὶ κοβαλικεύμασιν.

10. Jerks of style, from the lunatic trope, 'ῥήμαθ' ἱπποβάμονα, πολλάς τε ἀλινδήθρας ἐπῶν, to the buffoonery and "red-lattice phrases" of the Canaglia, Σκῶρ συσκεδῶν βόρβορον τε πολὺν καὶ κακίας καὶ συκοφαντίας; the one in ostentation of superior rank and acquirements (for where envy does

not interfere, man loves to *look up;*) the other in pledge of *heartiness* and good fellowship. 11. Lastly, and throughout all, to leave a general impression of something striking, *something that is to come of it,* and to rely on the indolence of mens' understandings and the activity of their passions for their resting in this state, as the *brood*-warmth fittest to hatch whatever serpents' egg opportunity may enable the Deceiver to place under it. Let but mysterious expressions* be aided by significant looks and tones, and you may cajole an hot and ignorant audience to believe any thing by saying nothing, and finally to act on the lie which they themselves have been drawn in to make. This is the Pharmacopœia of political empirics, here and everywhere, now and at all times! These are the drugs administered, and the tricks played

* Vide North's Examen, p. 20; and The Knights of Aristophanes. A version of this comedy, abridged and modernized, would be a most seasonable present to the Public. The words quoted above from this Play and the frogs, may be rendered freely in the order in which they occur: thus,

1. Thence he is illustrious, as a man of all waters, a bold fellow, and one who knows how to tickle the populace.

2. Phrases on horse-back, curvetting and careering words.

3. Scattering filth and dirt, malice and sycophantic tales.

off by the Mountebanks and Zanies of Patriotism; drugs that will continue to poison as long as irreligion secures a predisposition to their influence; and artifices, that like stratagems in war, are never the less successful for having succeeded a hundred times before. *"They bend their tongues as a bow; they shoot out deceits as arrows: they are prophets of the deceit of their own hearts: they cause the people to err by their dreams and their lightness: they make the people vain, they feed them with wormwood, they give them the water of gall for drink; and the people love to have it so. And what is the end thereof?* (JEREM. *passim.*)

The Prophet answers for me in the concluding words of the description—TO DESTROY THE POOR EVEN WHEN THE NEEDY SPEAKETH ARIGHT—that is, to impel them to acts that must end in their ruin by inflammatory falsehoods and by working on their passions till they lead them to reject the prior convictions of their own sober and unsophisticated understandings. As in all the preceding features so in this, with which the prophetic portrait is completed, our own experience supplies both proof and example. The ultimate causes of the present distress and stagnation are in the Writer's opinion complex and deeply seated; but the immediate occasion is too obvious to be over-looked but by eyes at once red and dim through the intoxication of factious prejudice, that maddening spirit which pre-eminently deserves the title of vinum dæmonum applied by an ancient Father of the Church to a far more innocent phrenzy. It is demonstrable that taxes, the product of which is circulated in the Country from which they are raised, can never injure a Country *directly* by the mere amount; but either from the time or circumstances under which they are raised, or from the injudicious mode in which they are levied, or from the improper objects to which they are applied. The Sun may draw up the moisture from the river, the morass, and the ocean, to be given back in genial showers to the garden, the pasture and the cornfield; but it may likewise force upward the moisture from the fields of industry to drop it on the stagnant pool, the saturated swamp, or the unprofitable sandwaste. The corruptions of a system can be duly appreciated by those only who have contemplated the system in that ideal state of perfection exhibited by the reason: the nearest possible approximation to which under existing circumstances it is the business of the prudential understanding to realize. Those on the other hand, who commence the examination of a system by identifying it with its abuses or imperfections, degrade their understanding into the pander of their passions, and are sure to prescribe remedies more dangerous than the disease. Alas! there are so many real evils, so many just causes of complaint in the constitutions and administration of all governments, our own not excepted, that it becomes the imperious duty of the true patriot to prevent, as much as in him lies, the feelings and efforts of his fellow country-men from losing themselves on a wrong scent.

If then we are to master the *Ideal* of a beneficent and judicious system of Finance as the preliminary to all profitable insight into the defects of any particular system in actual existence, we could not perhaps find an apter illustration than the gardens of southern Europe would supply. The tanks or reservoirs would represent the capital of a nation: while the hundred rills hourly varying their channels and directions, under the gardener's spade, would give a pleasing image of the dispersion of that capital through the whole population by the joint effect of taxation and trade. For taxation itself is a part of commerce, and the Government may be fairly considered as a great manufacturing-house, carrying on in different places, by means of its partners and overseers, the trades of the ship-builder, the clothier, the iron-founder, &c. &c. As long as a balance is preserved between the receipts and the returns of Government in their amount, quickness, and degree of dispersion; as long as the due proportion obtains in the sums levied to the mass in productive circulation, so long does the wealth and circumstantial prosperity of the nation, (its wealth, I say not its real welfare; its outward prosperity, but not necessarily its happiness) remain unaffected, or rather they will appear to increase in consequence of the additional stimulus given to the circulation itself by the productive action of all large capitals, and through the check which taxation, in its own nature, gives to the indolence of the wealthy in its continual transfer of property to the industrious and enterprizing.

If different periods be taken, and if the comparative weight of the taxes at each be calculated, as it ought to be, not by the sum *levied on* each individual, but by the sum *left in his possession,* the settlement of the account will be in favor of the national wealth, to the amount of all the additional productive labor sustained or excited by the taxes during the intervals between their efflux and their re-absorption.

But on the other hand, in a direct ratio to this increase will be the distress produced by the disturbance of this balance, by the loss of this proportion; and the operation of the distress will be at least equal to the total amount of the difference between the taxes still levied, and the quantum of aid withdrawn from individuals by the abandonment of others, and of that which the taxes, that still remain, have ceased to give by the altered mode of their re-dispersion. But to this we must add the number of persons raised and reared in consequence of the demand created by the preceding state of things, and now discharged from their occupations: whether the latter belong exclusively to the Executive Power, as that of soldiers, &c. or from those in which the laborers for the nation in general are already sufficiently numerous. Both these classes are thrown back on the Public, and sent to a table where every seat is pre-occupied. The employment lessens as the number of men to be employed is increased; and not merely in the same, but from additional causes and from the indirect consequences of those already stated, in a far greater ratio. For it may easily happen, that the very same change, which had produced this depression at home, may from equivalent causes have embarrassed the countries in commercial connection with us. At one and the same time the great customer at home wants less, and our customers abroad are able to buy less. The conjoint action of these circumstances will furnish, for a mind capable of combining them, a sufficient solution of the melancholy fact. They cannot but occasion much distress, much obstruction, and these again in their re-action are sure to be more than doubled by the still greater and universal alarm, and by the consequent check of confidence and enterprize, which they never fail to produce.

Now it is a notorious fact, that these causes

did all exist to a very extraordinary degree, and that they all worked with united strength, in the late sudden transition from War to Peace. It was one among the many anomalies of the late War, that it acted, after a few years, as a universal stimulant. We almost monopolized the commerce of the world. The high wages of our artisans and the high prices of agricultural produce intercirculated. Leases of no unusual length not seldom enabled the provident and thrifty farmer to purchase the estate he had rented. Every where might be seen roads, rail-ways, docks, canals, made, making, and projected; villages swelling into towns, while the metropolis surrounded itself, and became (as it were) *set* with new cities. Finally, in spite of all the waste and havoc of a twenty years' war, the population of the empire was increased by more than two millions! The efforts and war-expenditure of the nation, and the yearly revenue, were augmented in the same proportion: and to all this we must add a fact of the utmost importance in the present question, that the war did not, as was usually the case in former wars, die away into a long expected peace by gradual exhaustion and weariness on both sides, but *plunged* to its conclusion by a concentration, we might almost say, by a *spasm* of energy, and consequently by an *anticipation* of our resources. We conquered by compelling *reversionary* power into alliance with our existing and natural strength. The first intoxication of triumph having passed over, this our "agony of glory," was succeeded, of course, by a general stiffness and relaxation. The antagonist passions came into play; financial solicitude was blended with constitutional and political jealousies, and both, alas! were exacerbated by personal imprudences, the chief injury of which consisted in their own tendency to disgust and alienate the public feeling. And with all this, the financial errors and prejudices even of the more educated classes, in short, the general want or imperfection of clear views and a scientific insight into the true effects and influences of Taxation, and the mode of its operation, became now a real misfortune, and opened an additional source of temporary embarrassment. Retrenchment could no longer proceed by cautious and calculated steps; but was compelled to hurry forward, like one who crossing the sands at too late an hour finds himself threatened by the inrush of the tide. Nevertheless, it was a truth susceptible of little less than mathematical demonstration, that the more, and the more suddenly, the Revenue was diminished by the abandonment of the war-taxes, the greater would be the disturbance of the Balance:* so that the agriculturalist, the manufacturer, or the tradesman, (all in short but annuitants and fixed stipendiaries) who during the war having paid as Five had

* The disturbance of this balance may be illustrated thus:— Suppose a great Capitalist to have founded, in a large market-town, a factory that gradually increasing employed at length from five to six hundred workmen; and that he had likewise a second factory at a distance from the former (in the Isle of Man, for instance) employing half that number, all of the latter having been drafted from and still belonging to the first Parish. After some years we may further suppose, that a large proportion of the housekeepers and tradespeople might have a running account with the Capitalist, many with him, as being their landlord, and still more for their stock. The workmen would in like manner be for the greatest part on the books of the tradesfolks. As long as this state of things continued, all would go on well—nay, the town would be more prosperous with every increase of the factory. THE BALANCE IS PRESERVED. The circulations counterpoise each other, or rather they are neutralized by influence. But some sudden event leads or compels the Capitalist to put down both factories at once

Fifteen left behind, would shortly have less than Ten after having paid but Two and a Half.

But there is yet another circumstance, which we dare not pass by unnoticed. In the best of times—or what the world calls such—the spirit of commerce will occasion great fluctuations, some falling while others rise, and therefore in all times there will be a large sum of

and with little or no warning; and to call in all the moneys owing to him, and which by law had the preference to all other debts.—What would be the consequence? The workmen are no longer employed, and cannot at once pay up their arrears to the tradesmen; and though the Capitalist should furnish the latter with goods at half price, and make the same abatement in their rent, these deductions would afford little present relief: while in the meantime the discharged workmen from the distant factory would fall back on the Parish, and increase the general distress. THE BALANCE IS DISTURBED.—Put the Country at large for the parishioners, and the Government in all departments of expenditure for the Capitalist and his factories: and nearly such is the situation in which we are placed by the transition from the late War to the present Peace. But the difference is this. The Town may never recover its temporary prosperity, and the Capitalist may spend his remaining fortune in another country; but a nation, of which the Government is an organic part with perfect interdependence of interests, can never remain in a state of depression thus produced, but by its own fault: that is, from moral causes.

individual distress. Trades likewise have their seasons, and at all times there is a very considerable number of artificers who are not employed on the average more than seven or eight months in the year: and the distress from this cause is great or small in proportion to the greater or less degree of dissipation and improvidence prevailing among them. But besides this, that artificial life and vigor of Trade and Agriculture, which was produced or occasioned by the direct or indirect influences of the late War, proved by no means innoxious in its effects. Habit and the familiarity with outward advantages, which takes off their *dazzle;* sense of character; and above all, the counterpoise of intellectual pursuits and resources; are all necessary preventives and antidotes to the dangerous properties of wealth and power with the great majority of mankind. It is a painful subject: and I leave to your own experience and recollection the assemblage of folly, presumption, and extravagance, that followed in the procession of our late unprecedented prosperity; the blind practices and blending passions of speculation in the commercial world, with the shoal of ostentatious, fooleries and sensual vices which the sudden influx of wealth let in on our farmers and yeomanry. Now though the whole mass of calamity consequent on these aberrations from prudence should in all fairness be attributed to the sufferer's own conduct; yet when there supervenes some one common cause or occasion of distress which pressing hard on many furnishes a pretext to all, this too will pass muster among its actual effects, and assume the semblance and dignity of national calamity. Each unfortunate individual shares during *the hard times* in the immunities of a privileged order, as the most tottering and ruinous houses equally with those in best repair are included in the same brief after an extensive fire. The change of the moon will not produce a change of weather, except in places where the atmosphere has from local and particular causes been predisposed to its influence. But the former is one, placed aloft and conspicuous to all men; the latter are many and intricate, and known to few. Of course it is the moon that must bear the entire blame of wet summers and scanty crops. All these, however, whether they are distresses common to all times alike, or though *occasioned* by the general revolution and stagnation, yet really *caused* by personal improvidence or misconduct, combine with its peculiar and inevitable effects in making the cup overflow. The latter class especially, as being in such cases always the most clamorous sufferers, increase the evil by swelling the alarm.

The principal part of the preceding explication, the main causes of the present exigencies are so obvious, and lay so open to the common sense of mankind, that the laboring classes saw the connection of the change in the times with the suddenness of the peace, as clearly as their superiors, and being less heated with speculation, were in the first instance less surprized at the results. To a public event of universal concern there will often be more attributed than belongs to it; but never in the natural course of human feelings will there be less. That the depression began *with* the Peace would have been of itself a sufficient proof with the Many, that it arose *from* the Peace. But this opinion suited ill with the purposes of sedition. The truth, that could not be precluded, must be removed; and "*when the needy speaketh aright*" the more urgent occasion is there for the "*wicked device*" and the "*lying words.*" Where distress is felt, tales of wrong and oppression are readily believed, to the sufferer's own disquiet. Rage and Revenge make the cheek pale and the hand tremble, worse than even want itself: and the cup of sorrow overflows by being held unsteadily. On the other hand nothing calms the mind in the hour of bitterness so efficaciously as the conviction that it was not within the means of those above us, or around us, to have prevented it. An influence, mightier than fascination, dwells in the stern eye of necessity, when it is fixed steadily on a man: for together with the *power* of resistance it takes away its agitations likewise. This is one mercy that always accompanies the visitations of the Almighty when they are received *as* such. If therefore the sufferings of the lower classes are, to supply air and fuel to their passions, and are to be perverted into instruments of mischief, they must be attributed to causes that can be represented as removeable; either to individuals who had been previously rendered unpopular, or to whole classes of men, according as the immediate object of their seducers may require. What, though nothing should be more remote from the true cause? What though the invidious charge should be not only without proof, but in the face of strong proof to the contrary? What though the pretended remedy should have no possible end but that of exasperating the disease? All will be of little or no avail, if these truths have not been administered beforehand. When *the wrath is gone forth the plague is already begun:* (Numbers, xvi. 46.) *Wrath is cruel,* and where is there a deafness like that of an outrageous multitude? *For as the matter of the fire is, so it burneth.* Let the demagogue but succeed in maddening the crowd, he may bid defiance to demonstration, and direct the madness against whom it pleaseth him. *A slanderous tongue has disquieted many, and driven them from nation to nation; strong cities hath it pulled down and overthrown the houses of great men.* (Ecclesiasticus, xxviii. 14.)

We see in every promiscuous public meeting the effect produced by the bold assertion that the present hardships of all classes are owing to the number and amount of PENSIONS and SINE-CURES. Yet from the unprecedented zeal and activity in the education* of the poor, of the thousands that are inflamed by, and therefore give credit to, these statements, there are few without a child at home, who could

---

* With all due humility we contended that the war in question had likewise its *golden side*. The anomalous occasions and stupendous events of the contest had roused us, like the blast of a trumpet from the clouds; and as many as were capable of thinking were roused to thought. It had forced on the higher and middle classes—say rather on the people at large, as distinguished from the mere populace—the home truth, that national honesty and individual safety, private morals and public security, mutually grounded each other, that they were twined at the very root, and could not grow or thrive but in intertwine: and we of Great Britain had acquired this instruction without the stupifying influences of terror or actual calamity. Yet that it had operated practically, and in a scale proportional to the magnitude of the occasion, the late and present condition of manners and intellect among the young men at Oxford and Cambridge, the manly sobriety of demeanor, the submission to the routine of study in almost all, and the zeal in the pursuit of knowledge and academic distinction in a large and increasing number, afford a cheering testimony to such as were familiar with the state of the two Universities forty, or even thirty years ago, with the moral contrast which they presented, at the close of the last, and during the former half of the present reign; while a proof of still greater power, and open to the observation of all men, is supplied by the predominant anxiety concerning the education and principles of their children in all the respectable classes

prove their impossibility by the first and simplest rules of arithmetic; there is not one perhaps, who taken by himself and in a cooler mood, would stand out against the simple question: whether it was not folly to suppose that the lowness of his wages, or his want of employment could be occasioned by the cir-

of the community, and the unexampled sale, in consequence, of the very numerous large and small volumes composed or compiled for the use of parents. Nor here did the salutary influence stop. We had been compelled to know and feel that the times in which we had to act or suffer were the saturnalia of revolution; and fearful evidence had been given us at the cost of our unfortunate neighbours, that a vicious and ignorant population was a magazine of combustibles left rootless, while madmen and incendiaries were letting off their new invented blue lights and fire-rockets in every direction. The wish sprang up and spread throughout England that every Englishman should be able to read his Bible and have a Bible of his own to read. The general wish organized itself into act and plan: a discovery, the living educt of one great man's genius and benevolence, rendered the execution practicable and even easy; and the god-like idea began and is proceeding to realize itself with a rapidity yet stedfastness which nothing could make possible or credible but such a conviction effected by an experience so strange and awful, and acting on that volunteer spirit, that instinct of fervid yet orderly co-operation, which most of all our honourable characteristics distinguishes, secures, enriches, strengthens and elevates the people of Great Britain. [*From an Essay by the Author, published in the Courier, July*, 1816.]

cumstances, that a sum (the whole of which, as far as it is raised by taxation, cannot take a yearly penny from him) was dispersed and returned into the general circulation by Annuitants of the Treasury instead of Annuitants of the Bank, by John instead of Peter: however blameable the regulation might be in other respects? What then? the hypothesis allows of a continual reference to *persons*, and to all the uneasy and malignant passions which personalities are of all means the best fitted to awaken. The *grief* itself, however grinding it may be, is of no avail to this end; it must be first converted into a *grievance*. Were the audience composed chiefly of the lower Farmers and the Peasantry, the same circumstance would for the same reason have been attributed wholly to the Clergy and the system of TYTHES; as if the corn would be more plentiful if the Farmers paid their whole rent to one man, instead of paying nine parts to the Landlords and the tenth to the Tythe-owners! But let the meeting be composed of the Manufacturing Poor, and then it is the MACHINERY of their employers that is devoted to destruction: though it would not exceed the truth if I affirmed, that to the use and perfection of this very Machinery the majority of the poor deluded destroyers owe their very *existence,* owe to it that they ever beheld the light of heaven!

Even so it is with the Capitalists and Storekeepers, who by spreading the dearness of provisions over a larger space and time prevent scarcity from becoming real famine, the frightful lot at certain and not distant intervals of our less commercial forefathers. These men by the mere instinct of self-interest are not alone birds of warning, that prevent waste; but as the raven of Elijah, they bring supplies from afar. But let the incendiary spirit have rendered them birds of ill omen: and it is well if the deluded Malcontents can be restrained from levelling at them missiles more alarming than the curse of the unwise that alighteth not. *There be three things* (says the wise son of Sirach) *that mine heart feareth, the slander of a city, the gathering together of an unruly multitude, and a false accusation: all these are worse than death.* But all these are the Arena, and the chosen weapons of demagogues. Wretches! they would without remorse detract the hope that is the subliming and expanding warmth of public credit, destroy the public credit that is the vital air of national industry, convert obstruction into stagnation, and make grass grow in the exchange and the market-place; if so they might but goad ignorance into riot, and fanaticism into rebellion! They would snatch the last morsel from the poor man's lips to make him curse the Government in his heart—alas! to fall at length, either ignominiously beneath the *strength* of the outraged Law, or (if God in his anger, and for the punishment of general depravity should require a severer and more extensive retribution) to perish still more lamentably among the victims of its *weakness*.

Thus then, I have answered at large to the first of the three questions proposed as the heads and divisions of this Address. I am well aware that our demagogues are not the only empirics who have tampered with the case. But I felt unwilling to put the mistakes of sciolism, or even those of vanity and self-interest, in the same section with crime and guilt. What is omitted here will find its place elsewhere; the more readily, that having been tempted by the foulness of the ways to turn for a short space out of my direct path, I have encroached already on the second question; that, namely, which respects the ultimate causes and immediate occasions of the complaint.

The latter part of this problem I appear to myself to have solved fully and satisfactorily. To those who deem any further or deeper research superfluous, I must content myself with observing, that I have never heard it denied, that there is more than a sufficiency of food in existence. I have, at least, met with no proof that there is, or has been any scarcity, either in the materials of all necessary comforts, or any lack of strength, skill and industry to prepare them. If we saw a man in health pining at a full table because there was not 'the savory meat there which he loved,' and had expected, the wanton delay or negligence of the messenger would be a complete answer to our enquiries after the *occasion* of this sullenness or inappetence; but the *cause* of it we should be tempted to seek in the man's own undisciplined temper, or habits of self-indulgence. So far from agreeing therefore with those who find the causes in the occasions, I think the half of the question already solved of every unequal importance with that which yet remains for solution.

The immediate occasions of the existing distress may be correctly given with no greater difficulty than would attend any other series of known historic facts; but toward the discovery of its true seat and sources, I can but offer a humble contribution. They appear to me, however, resolvable into the OVERBALANCE* OF THE COMMERCIAL SPIRIT IN CONSEQUENCE OF THE ABSENCE OR WEAKNESS OF THE COUNTER-WEIGHTS; this overbalance considered as displaying itself, 1. In the COMMERCIAL

---

* I entreat attention to the word, *over*-balance. My opinions would be greatly misinterpreted if I were supposed to think hostilely of the spirit of commerce to which I attribute the largest proportion of our actual freedom (i. e. as *Englishmen*, and not merely as *Landowners*) and at least as large a share of our virtues as of our vices. Still more anxiously would I guard against the suspicion of a design to inculpate any number or class of individuals. It is not in the power of a minister or of a cabinet to say to the current of national tendency, stay here! or flow there! The excess can only be remedied by the slow progress of intellect, the influences of religion, and irresistible events guided by Providence. In the points even, which I have presumed to blame, by the word Government I intend all the directors of political power, that is, the great estates of the Realm, temporal and spiritual, and not only the Parliament, but all the elements of Parliament.

WORLD itself: 2. In the Agricultural: 3. In the Government: and 4. In the combined Influence of all three on the more numerous and labouring Classes.

Of the natural counter-forces to the impetus of trade the first, that presents itself to my mind, is the ancient feeling of rank and ancestry, compared with our present self-complacent triumph over these supposed prejudices. Not that titles and the rights of precedence are pursued by us with less eagerness than by our Forefathers. The contrary is the case; and for this very cause, because they inspire less reverence. In the old times they were valued by the possessors and revered by the people as distinctions of *Nature*, which the crown itself could only ornament, but not give. Like the stars in Heaven, their influence was wider and more general, because for the mass of mankind there was no hope of reaching, and therefore no desire to appropriate, them. That many evils as well as advantages accompanied this state of things I am well aware: and likewise that many of the latter* have become incompatible with far more important blessings. It would therefore be sickly affectation to suspend the thankfulness due for our immunity from the one in an idle regret for the loss of the other. But however true this may be, and whether the good or the evil proponderated, still it acted as a counterpoise to the grosser superstition for wealth. Of the efficiency of this counter-influence we can offer negative proof only: and for this we need only look back on the deplorable state of Holland in respect of patriotism and public spirit at and before the commencement of the French revolution.

The limits and proportions of this address allow little more than a bare reference to this point. The same restraint I must impose on myself in the following. For under this head I conclude the general neglect of all the austerer studies; the long and ominous eclipse of Philosophy; the usurpation of that venerable name by physical and psychological Empiricism; and the non-existence of a learned and philosophic Public, which is perhaps the only innoxious form of an imperium in imperio, but at the same time the only form which is not directly or indirectly encouraged. So great a risk do I incur of malignant interpretation, and the assertion itself is so likely to appear paradoxical even to men of candid minds, that I should have passed over this point, most important as I know it to be; but that it will be found stated more at large, with all its proofs, in a work on the point of publication. The fact is simply this. We have—*Lovers*, shall I entitle them? Or must I not rather hazard the introduction of their own phrases, and say, *Amateurs* or *Dillettanti*, as Musicians, Botanists, Florists, Mineralogists, and Antiquarians. Nor is it denied that these are ingenuous pursuits, and such as become men of rank and fortune. Neither in these or in any other points do I complain of any excess in the pursuits themselves; but of that which arises from the deficiency of the counterpoise. The effect is the same. Every work, which can be made use of either to immediate profit or immediate pleasure, every work which falls in with the desire of acquiring wealth suddenly, or which can gratify the senses, or pamper the still more degrading appetite for scandal and personal defamation, is sure of an appropriate circulation. But neither Philosophy or Theology in the strictest sense of the words, can be said to have even a public *existence* among us. I feel assured, that if Plato himself were to return and renew his sublime lucubrations in the metropolis of Great Britain, a handicraftsman, from a laboratory, who had just succeeded in disoxydating an Earth, would be thought far the more respectable, nay, the more illustrious person of the two. Nor will it be the least drawback from his honors, that he had never even asked himself, what law of universal Being Nature uttered in this phænomenon: while the character of a visionary would be the sole remuneration of the man, who from the insight into that law had previously demonstrated the necessity of the fact. As to that which passes with us under the name of metaphysics, philosophic elements, and the like, I refer every man of reflection to the contrast between the present times and those shortly after the restoration of ancient literature. In the latter we find the greatest men of the age, Statesmen, Warriors, Monarchs, Architects, in closest intercourse with philosophy. I need only mention the names of Lorenzo the magnificent; Picus, Count Mirandula, Ficinus and Politian; the abstruse subjects of their discussion, and the importance attached to them, as the requisite qualifications of men placed by Providence as guides and governors of their fellow-creatures. If this be undeniable, equally notorious is it that at present the more effective a man's talents are, and the more likely he is to be useful and distinguished in the highest situations of public life, the earlier does he shew his aversion to the metaphysics and the books of metaphysical speculation, which are placed before him: though they come with the recommendation of being so many triumphs of modern good sense over the schools of ancient philosophy. Dante, Petrarch, Spencer, Sir Philip Sidney, Algernon Sidney, Milton and Barrow were Platonists. But all the men of genius, with whom it has been my fortune to converse, either profess to know nothing of the present systems, or to despise them. It would be equally unjust and irrational to seek the solution of this difference in the men; and if not, it can be found only in the philosophic systems themselves. And so in truth it is. The *Living* of former ages communed gladly with a life-breathing philosophy. The *Living* of the present age wisely leave the dead to take care of the dead.

But whatever the causes may be, the result is before our eyes. An excess in our attachment to temporal and personal objects can be counteracted only by a pre-occupation of the intellect and the affections with permanent, universal, and eternal truths. Let no man enter, said Plato, who has not previously disciplined his mind by Geometry. He considered this science as the first purification of the soul, by abstracting the attention from the accidents of the senses. We too teach Geometry; but that there may be no danger of the pupil's becoming too *abstract* in his conceptions, it has been not only proposed, but the proposal has been adopted, that it should be taught by *wooden diagrams!* It pains me to remember with what applause a work, that placed the inductions of modern Chemistry in the same rank with the demonstrations of Mathematical Science, was received even in a mathematical University. I must not permit myself to say more on this subject, desirous as I am of shewing the importance of a philosophic class, and of evincing that it is of vital utility, and even an essential element in the composition of a civilized community. It must suffice, that it has been explained in what respect the pursuit of Truth for its own sake, and the reverence yielded to its professors, has a tendency to calm or counteract the pursuit of wealth; and that therefore a counterforce is wanting wherever Philosophy is degraded in the estimation of society. What are *you* (a philosopher was once asked) in consequence of your admiration of these abstruse speculations? He answered: What I am, it does not become me to say; but what thousands are, who despise them, and even pride themselves on their ignorance, I see—and tremble!

There is a third influence, alternately our spur and our curb, without which all the pursuits and desires of man must either exceed or fall short of their just measure. Need I add, that I mean the influence of Religion? I speak of that sincere, that entire interest, in the undivided faith of Christ which demands the first-fruits of the whole man, his affections no less than his outward acts, his understanding equally with his feelings. For be assured, never yet did there exist a full faith in the divine WORD, (by whom not Immortality alone, but *Light* and Immortality were brought into the world) which did not expand the intellect while it purified the heart; which did not multiply the aims and objects of the mind, while it fixed and simplified those of the desires and passions. If acquiescence without insight; if warmth without light; if an immunity from doubt given and guaranteed by a resolute ignorance; if the habit of taking for granted the words of a catechism, remembered or forgotten; if a sensation of *positiveness* substituted—I will not say, for certainty; but—for that calm assurance, the very means and conditions of which it supersedes; if a belief that seeks the darkness, and yet strikes no root, immovable as the limpet from its rock, and like the limpet fixed there by mere force of adhesion; if these suffice to make us Christians, in what intelligible sense could our Lord have announced it as the height and consummation of the signs and *miracles* which attested his Divinity, that the Gospel was preached to the POOR? In what sense could the Apostle affirm, that Believers have received, not indeed the wisdom of this world that comes to nought, but the wisdom of God, that we might know and comprehend the things that are freely given to us of God? or that every Christian, in proportion as he is indeed a Christian, has received the Spirit that *searcheth* all things, yea the deep things of God himself?—on what grounds could the Apostle denounce even the sincerest fervor of spirit as defective, where it does not bring forth fruits in the *Understanding?** Or again: if to believe were enough, why are we commanded by another Apostle, that, "besides this, giving all diligence we should add to our faith manly energy and to manly energy *knowledge!*" Is it not especially significant, that in the divine œconomy, as revealed to us in the New Testament, the peculiar office of Redemption is attributed to the WORD, that is, to the *intelligential* wisdom which from all eternity is with God, and is God? that in *him* is life, and the life is the *light* of men?

In the present day we hear much, and from men of various creeds, of the *plainness* and *simplicity* of the Christian religion: and strange abuse has been made of these words, often indeed with no ill intention, but still oftener by men who would fain transform the necessity of

---

* Brethren! be not children in understanding: howbeit, in malice be ye children, but in understanding be men.

believing *in* Christ into a recommendation to believe him. The advocates of the latter scheme grew out of a sect that were called Socinians, but having succeeded in disbelieving far beyond the last foot-marks of the Socini, have chosen to designate themselves by the name of *Unitarians*. But this is a word, which in its proper sense, can belong only to their antagonists: for Unity or Unition, and indistinguishable *Unicity* or Oneness, are incompatible terms: while, in the exclusive sense in which they mean the name to be understood, it is a presumptuous boast, and an uncharitable calumny. Their true designation, which simply expresses a fact admitted on all sides, would be that of *Psilanthropists*,* or assertors of the *mere* humanity of Christ. It is the interest of these men to speak of the Christian reli-

---

* New things justify new terms. Novis in rebus licet nova nobis verba confingere.—We never speak of the *unity* of Attraction, or of the unity of Repulsion; but of the unity of Attraction and Repulsion in each one corpuscle. The essential diversity of the ideas, unity and sameness, was among the elementary principles of the old Logicians; and the sophisms grounded on the confusion of these terms have been ably exposed by Leibnitz, in his Critique on Wissowatius, the acutest, perhaps, of all the learned Socinian divines, when Socinian divines were undeniably men of learning.

gion as comprized in a few plain doctrines, and containing nothing not intelligible, at the first hearing, to men of the narrowest capacities. Well then, (it might be replied) we are disposed to place a full reliance on the veracity of the great Founder of the Christian Religion, and likewise—which is more than you yourselves are on all occasions willing to admit—on the accuracy and competence of the Writers, who first recorded his acts and sayings. We have learned from you, *whom*,—and we now wish to hear from you—*what* we are to believe. The answer is:—the actural occurrence of an extraordinary event, as recorded by the biographers of Jesus, in confirmation of doctrines, without the *previous* belief of which, no man would, or rather, according to St. Paul's declaration, *could* become a convert to Christianity; doctrines, which it is certain, that Christ's immediate disciples believed, not less confidently before they had acknowledged his mission, than they did afterwards. Religion and politics, they tell us, require but the application of a common sense, which every man possesses, to a subject in which every man is concerned. "To be a musician, an orator, a painter, or even a good mechanician, pre-supposes *genius*; to be an excellent artizan or mechanic requires more than an average degree of *talent*; but to be a legislator or a theologian, or both at once, demands nothing but common sense."* Now we willingly admit that nothing can be necessary to the salvation of a Christian which is not in his power. For such, therefore, as have neither the opportunity or the capacity of learning more, sufficient, doubtless, will be the belief of those plain truths, and the fulfilment of those commands, which to be incapable of understanding, is to be a man in appearance only. But even to this scanty creed the *disposition* of faith must be added: and let it not be forgotten, that though nothing can be easier than to understand a code of belief, four-fifths of which consists in avowals of disbelief, and the remainder in truths, concerning which (in this country at least) a man must have *taken pains*

---

* THE FRIEND, Vol. I. As the original work, of which but a small number of copies were printed on stamped sheets, and sent to the subscribers by the post, is not to be procured; the reference is made to the edition now printing, in three volumes, of the size of the British Essayists: if indeed a work, a great part of which is new in substance, and the whole in form and arrangement, can be described as an edition of the former.

to learn to have any doubt; yet it is by no means easy to reconcile this code of negatives with the declarations of the Christian Scripture. On the contrary, it requires all the resources of verbal criticism, and all the perverse subtlety of special pleading, to work out a plausible semblance of correspondency between them. It must, however, be conceded, that a man may consistently spare himself the trouble of the attempt, and leave the New Testament unread, after he has once thoroughly persuaded himself that it can teach him nothing of any real importance that he does not already know. St. Paul indeed thought otherwise. For though he too teaches us, that in the religion of Christ there is milk for babes; yet he informs us at the same time, that there is meat for strong men! and to the like purpose one of the Fathers has observed, that in the New Testament there are shallows where the lamb may ford, and depths where the elephant must swim. The Apostle exhorts the followers of Christ to the continual study of the new religion, on the ground that in the mystery of Christ, which in other ages was not made known to the sons of men, and in the riches of Christ which no research could exhaust, there were contained all the treasures of knowledge and wisdom. Accordingly, in that earnestness of spirit, which his own personal experience of the inspired truth, he prays with a solemn and a ceremonious fervor, that being "strengthened with might in the inner man, they may be able to comprehend with all saints what is the breadth and length and depth and height," of that living Principle, at once the Giver and the Gift! of that anointing Faith, which in endless evolution "*teaches us of all things, and is truth!*" For all things are but parts and forms of its progressive manifestation, and every new knowledge but a new organ of sense and insight into this one all-inclusive Verity, which, still filling the vessel of the understanding, still dilates it to a capacity of yet other and yet greater Truths, and thus makes the soul feel its poverty by the very amplitude of its present, and the immensity of its reversionary, wealth. All truth indeed is simple, and needs no extrinsic ornament. And the more profound the truth is, the more simple: for the whole labour and building-up of knowledge is but one continued process of simplification. But I cannot comprehend, in what ordinary sense of the words the properties of *plainness* and *simplicity* can be applied to the Prophets, or to the Writings of St. John, or to the Epistles of St. Paul; or what can have so marvellously improved the capacity of *our* laity beyond the same class of persons among the primitive Christians; who, as we are told by a fellow apostle, found in the Writings last-mentioned many passages hard to be understood, which the *unlearned*, as well as the unstable, were in danger of wresting and misinterpreting. I can well understand, however, what is and has been the practical consequence of this notion. It is this very consequence indeed, that occasioned the preceding remarks, makes them pertinent to my present subject, and gives them a place in the train of argument requisite for its illustration. For what need of any after-recurrence to the sources of information concerning a religion, the whole contents of which can be thoroughly acquired at once, and in a few hours? An occasional *remembrancing* may, perhaps, be expedient; but what object of *study* can a man propose to himself in a matter of which he knows all that can be known, all at least, that it is for us to know? Like the first rules of arithmetic, its few plain and obvious truths may hourly serve the man's purposes, yet never once occupy his thoughts. But it is impossible that the affections should be kept constant to an object which gives no employment to the understanding. The energies of the intellect, increase of insight, and enlarging views, are necessary to keep alive the substantial faith in the heart. They are the appointed fuel to the sacred fire. In the state of *Perfection* all other faculties may, perhaps, be swallowed up in love; but it is on the wings of the *Cherubim*, which the ancient Hebrew Doctors interpreted as meaning the powers and efforts of the Intellect, that we must first be borne up to the "pure Empyrean:" and it must be Seraphs and not the hearts of poor Mortals, that can burn unfuelled and self-fed. "Give me *understanding* (exclaimed the royal Psalmist) and I shall observe thy law with my whole heart. Teach me *knowledge* and good *judgment*. Thy commandment is exceeding *broad:* O how I love thy law! it is my *meditation* all the day. The entrance of thy words giveth *light*, it giveth *understanding* to the simple. I prevented the dawning of the morning: mine eyes prevent the night-watches, that I might meditate upon thy word." Now where the very contrary of this is the opinion of many, and the practice of most, what results can be expected but those which are actually presented to us in our daily experience.

There is one class of men* who read the Scriptures, when they do read them, in order to pick and choose their faith; or (to speak more accurately) for the purpose of plucking away *live-asunder,* as it were, from the divine organism of the Bible, textuary morsels and fragments for the support of doctrines which they

---

* Whether it be on the increase, as a Sect, is doubtful. But it is admitted by all—nay, strange as it may seem, made a matter of boast,—that the number of its secret adherents, outwardly of other denominations, is tenfold greater than that of its avowed and incorporated Followers. And truly, in our cities and great manufacturing and commercial towns, among Lawyers and such of the Tradesfolk as are the ruling members in Book-clubs, I am inclined to fear that this has not been asserted without good ground. For Socinianism in its present form, consisting almost wholly in attack and imagined detection, has a particular charm for what are called *shrewd, knowing* men. Besides, the vain and half-educated, whose Christian and sir names in the title pages of our Magazines, Lady's Diaries, &c. are the successors of the shame-faced Critos, Phileleutheroses, and Philaletheses in the time of our Grand-

had learned beforehand from the higher oracle *of their own natural Common-Sense. Sanctas Scripturas frustant ut frustrent.* Through the gracious dispensations of Providence a complexity of circumstances may co-operate as antidotes to a noxious principle, and realize the paradox of a very good man under a very evil faith. It is not denied, that a Socinian may be as honest, useful and benevolent a character as any of his neighbours; and if he *thinks* more and derives a larger portion of his pleasures from intellectual sources, he is likely to be more so. But in such instances, and I am most willing to bear witness from my own experience,

---

fathers, will be *something:* and now that Deism has gone out of fashion, Socinianism has swept up its Refuse. As the main success of this sect is owing to the small proportion which the affirmative articles of their Faith *(rari nantes in gurgite vasto)* bear to the negative, (that is, their Belief to their Disbelief, it will be an act of kindness to the unwary to bring together the former under one point of view. This is done in the following Catalogue, the greater part if not the whole of which may be authenticated from the writings of Mr. Belsham.

1. They believe in one God, professing to differ from other Christians only in holding the Deity to be unipersonal, the Father alone being God, the Son a mere, though an inspired and highly gifted, man, and the Holy Spirit either a Synonime of God, or of the divine agency, or of its effects.

2. They believe men's actions necessitated, and consistently

that they are not infrequent, the fruit is from the grafts not from the tree. The native produce is, or would be, an intriguing, overbearing, scornful and worldly disposition; and in point of fact, it is the only scheme of Religion that inspires in its adherents a contempt for the understandings of all who differ from them. But be this as it may, and whatever be its effects, it is not probable that Christianity will have any *direct* influence on men who pay it no other compliment than that of calling by its name the previous dictates and decisions of their own mother-wit.

But the more numerous class is of those

---

with this affirm that the Christian Religion (i. e. *their* view of it) precludes all *remorse* for our sins, they being a present calamity, but not *guilt*.

3. They believe the Gospels, though not written by inspiration, to be authentic Histories on the whole: though with some additions and interpolations. And on the authority of these Writings, confirmed by other evidence, they believe in the Resurrection of the Man, Jesus Christ, from the dead.

4. On the historic credibility of this event they believe in the Resurrection of the Body, which in their opinion is the Whole Man, at the last Day: and differ from other Churches in this only, that while other Christians believe, that all Men will arise in the Body, they hold, that all the Bodies that had been Men, will arise.

who do not trouble themselves at all with religious matters, which they resign to the clergyman of the parish. But while not a few among these men consent to pray and hear by proxy; and while others, more attentive to the prudential advantages of a decorous character, yield the customary evidence of their church-membership; but, this performed, are at peace with themselves, and

>———think their Sunday's task.
> As much as God or Man can fairly ask;

there exists amongst the most respectable Laity of our cities and great towns, an active,

---

5. A certain indefinite number of Mankind thus renewed to life and consciousness, it is the common belief of *them all*, will be placed in a state of happiness and immortality. But with respect to those who have died in the calamitous condition of unreformed Sinfulness, (to what extent it is for the supreme Judge to decide) they are divided among themselves. The one party teach, that such unhappy persons will be raised only to be re-annihilated: the other party contend, that there will be a *final* Restoration of all Men, with a purgatory or state of remedial discipline, the severity and duration of which will be proportioned to the kind, degree, and obstinacy of the Disease, and of which therefore every Man is left to his own conjectural Hopes and Fears: with this comfort however to the very worst, (i. e. most *unfortunate* and *erroneous* of Mankind) that it will be all well with them at last. In this article they

powerful, and enlarging minority, whose industry, while it enriches their families, is at the same time a support to the revenue, and not seldom enlivens their whole neighbourhood: men whose lives are free from all disreputable infirmities, and of whose activity in the organization, patronage, and management both of charitable and of religious associations, who must not have read or heard? and who that has, will dare deny to be most exemplary? After the custom of our forefathers, and their pure house-hold religion,* these, in so many

---

* And pure Religion breathing household laws.
WORDSWORTH.

differ from the Papists, in having no Hell, and in placing their Purgatory *after*, instead of before, the Day of Judgment.

6. Lastly, as they hold only an intellectual and physical, and not a *moral* difference in the actions and characters of Men, they not being free Agents, and therefore not more *responsible* Beings than the Brute Beasts, although their greater powers of memory and comparison render them more susceptible of being *acted on* by prospective motives—(and in *this* sense they retain the *term*, responsibility, after having purified it by the ex-inanition of its old, and the transfusion of a new, meaning) —and as they, with strict consequence, merge all the attributes of Deity in Power, Intelligence, and Benevolence, (Mercy and Justice being modes, or rather perspective views, of the two latter; the Holiness of God meaning the same or nothing at all; and his Anger, Offence, and Hatred, of Moral Evil, being

respects estimable persons, are for the greater part in the habit of having family-prayer, and a portion of Scripture read every morning and evening. In this class, with such changes or substitutions as the peculiar tenets of the sect require, we must include the sensible, orderly and beneficent Society of the FRIENDS, more commonly called Quakers. Here then, if any where, (that is, in any *class* of men; for the present argument is not concerned with individuals) we may expect to find Christianity tempering commercial avidity and sprinkling its holy damps on the passion of accumulation. This, I say, we might expect to find, if an un-

---

mere metaphors and figures of speech addressed to a rude and barbarous People) they profess to hold a Redemption—not however by the Cross of Christ, except as his death was an evidence of his sincerity, and the necessary preliminary to his Resurrection; but—by the effects which this fact of his Resurrection, together with his example, and his re-publication of the moral precepts (taught indeed long before, but *as they* think, not so clearly, by Moses and the Prophets) were calculated to produce on the human mind. So that if it had so happened, that a man had been influenced to an innocent and useful life by the example, precepts, and martyrdom of Socrates, Socrates and not Christ, would have been his Redeemer.

These are all the Positives of the modern Socinian Creed, and even these it was not possible to extricate wholly from the points of Disbelief. But if it should be asked, why this doubting belief in the threats and promises of Revelation, and a consequent regularity of personal, domestic, and social demeanor, sufficed to constitute that Christianity, the power and privilege of which is so to renew and irridiate the whole intelligential and moral life of man, as to overcome the *spirit of the world.* (St. John: Epistle I.) If this, the appointed test, were found wanting, should we not be forced to apprehend, nay, are we not compelled to infer, that the spirit of prudential motive, however ennobled by the magnitude and awfulness of its objects, and though as the termination of a lower, it may be the commencement (and not

---

resurrection, or re-creation is confined to the human animal, the answer must be—that more than this has not been revealed. And so far all Christians will join assent. But some have added, and in my opinion much to their credit, that they hope, it may be the case with the Brutes likewise, as they see no sufficient reason to the contrary. And truly, upon *their* scheme, I agree with them. For if a Man be no other or nobler Creature *essentially*, than he is represented in their system, the meanest reptile, that maps out its path on the earth by lines of slime, must be of equal worth and respectability, not only in the sight of the Holy One, but by a strange contradiction even before Man's own reason. For remove all the sources of Esteem and the Love founded on esteem, and whatever else pre-supposes a Will and, therein, a possible transcendence to the material world: Mankind, as far as my experience has

seldom the *occasion*) of an higher state, is not, even in respect of *morality* itself, that abiding and continuous principle of action, which is either *one* with the faith spoken of by St. Paul, or its immediate offspring. It cannot be that *spirit* of obedience to the commands of Christ, by which the soul dwelleth in him, and he in it: (1 John, c. iii. 4.) and which our Saviour himself announces as a *being born again.* And this indispensable act, or influence, or impregnation, of which, as of a divine tradition, the eldest philosophy is not silent; which flashed through the darkness of the pagan mysteries; and which it was therefore a reproach to a

extended, (and I am less than the least of many whom I could cite as having formed the very same judgment) are *on the whole* distinguished from the other Beasts incomparably more to their *disadvantage*, by Lying, Treachery, Ingratitude, Massacre, Thirst of Blood, and by Sensualities which both in sort and degree it would be libelling their Brother-beasts to call *bestial*, than to their advantage by a greater extent of Intellect. And what indeed, abstracted from the Free-will, could this intellect be but a more shewy instinct? of more various application indeed, but far less secure, useful, or adapted to its purposes, than the instinct of Birds, Insects, and the like. In short, as I have elsewhere observed, compared with the wiles and factories of the Spider, or with the cunning of the Fox, it would be but a more efflorescent, and for that very cause a

Master in Israel, that he had not already known; (John's Gospel, c. iii.)—this is elsewhere explained, as a seed which, though of gradual developement, did yet *potentially* contain the essential form not merely of a better, but of an *other* life: amidst all the frailties and transient eclipses of mortality making, I repeat, the subjects of this regeneration not so properly better as *other* men, whom therefore the world could not but hate, as aliens. Its own native growth, however, improved by cultivation (whether thro' the agency of blind symyathies, or of an intelligent self-interest, the utmost heights to which the *worldly life* can ascend)

less efficient, *Salt* to preserve the Hog from putrifying before its destined hour.

Well may the words of Isaiah be applied and addressed to the Teachers and Followers of this Sect, or rather, I would say, to their Tenets as personified—"The word of the Lord was unto them, precept upon precept, line upon line, here a little and there a little, that they might go and fall backward, and be broken and spared. Wherefore, hear the word of the Lord, ye *Scornful* Men that rule this people! Because ye have said, *We* have made a covenant with Death, and with Hell are *we* at agreement! Your Covenant with Death shall be annulled, and your agreement with Hell shall not stand. For your Bed is shorter than that a man can stretch himself upon it, and the covering narrower than that he can wrap himself in it."
Isaiah xxviii.

the World has always been ready and willing to acknowledge and admire. *They are of the world: therefore speak they out of the heart of the world* (ἐκ τοῦ κόσμου) *and the world heareth them.* (1 John, ivth.)

To abstain from acts of wrong and violence, to be moreover industrious, useful, and of seemly bearing, are qualities presupposed in the gospel code, as the preliminary conditions, rather than the proper and peculiar effects, of Christianity. But they are likewise qualities so palpably indispensable to the temporal interests of mankind that, if we except the brief frenzies of revolutionary Riot, there never was a time, in which the World did not profess to reverence them: nor can we state any period, in which a more than ordinary character for assiduity, regularity, and charitableness did not secure the World's praise and favor, and were not calculated to advance the individuals own worldly interests: provided only, that his manners and professed tenets were those of some known and allowed body of men.

I ask then, what is the fact? We are—and, till it's good purposes, which are many, have been all atchieved, and we can become something better, long may we continue such! —a busy, enterprizing, and commercial nation. The habits attached to this character must, if there exist no adequate counterpoise, inevitably lead us, under the specious names of utility, practical knowledge, and so forth, to look at all things thro' the medium of the market, and to estimate the Worth of all pursuits and attainments by their marketable value. In this does the Spirit of Trade consist. Now would the general experience bear us out in the assertion, that amid the absence or declension of all other antagonist Forces, there is found in the very circle of the trading and opulent themselves, in the increase, namely, of religious professors among them, a spring of resistance to the excess of the commercial impetus, from the impressive example of *their* unworldly feelings evidenced by *their* moderation in worldly pursuits? I fear, that we may anticipate the answer wherever the religious zeal of such professors does not likewise manifest itself by the glad devotion of as large a portion of their Time and Industry, as the duty of providing a fair competence for themselves and their families leaves at their own disposal, to the comprehension of those inspired writings and the evolution of those pregnant truths, which are proposed for our earnest, sedulous research, in order that by occupying our understandings they may more and more assimilate our affections? I fear, that the inquiring traveller would more often hear of zealous Religionists who have read (and as a duty too and with all due acquiescence) the prophetic, "Wo to them that join house to house and lay field to field, that they may be alone in the land!" and yet find no object deform the beauty of the prospect from their window or even from their castle turrets so annoyingly, as a meadow not their own, or a field under ploughing with the beam-end of the plough in the hands of its humble owner! I fear, that he must too often make report of men lawful in their dealings, scriptural in their language, alms-givers, and patrons of Sunday schools, who are yet resistless and overawing Bidders at all Land Auctions in their neighbourhood, who live in the center of farms without leases, and tenants without attachments! Or if his way should lie through our great towns and manufacturing districts, instances would grow cheap with him of wealthy religious practitioners, who never travel for orders without cards of edification in prose and verse, and small tracts of admonition and instruction, all "plain and easy, and suited to the meanest capacities;" who pray daily, as the first act of the morning and as the last of the evening, Lead us not into temptation! but deliver us from evil! and employ all the interval with an edge of appetite keen as the scythe of Death in the pursuit of yet more and yet more of a temptation so perilous, that (as they have full often read, and heard read, without the least questioning, or whisper of doubt) no power short of Omnipotence could make their deliverance from it credible or conceivable. Of all denominations of Christians, there is not one in existence or on record whose whole scheme of faith and worship was so expressly framed for the one purpose of spiritualizing the mind and of abstracting it from the vanities of the world, as the Society of Friends! not one, in which the church members are connected, and their professed principles enforced, by so effective and wonderful a form of discipline. But in the zeal of their Founders and first Proselytes for perfect Spirituality they excluded from their system all ministers specially trained and educated for the ministry, with all Professional Theologians: and they omitted to provide for the raising up among themselves any other established class of learned men, as teachers and schoolmasters for instance, in their stead. Even at this day, though the Quakers are in general remarkably shrewd and intelligent in all worldly concerns, yet learning, and more particularly theological learning, is more rare among them in proportion to their wealth and rank in life, and held in less value, than among any other known sect of Christians. What has been the result? If the occasion permitted, I could dilate with pleasure on their decent manners and decorous morals, as individuals, and their exemplary and truly illustrious philanthropic efforts as a Body. From all the gayer and tinsel vanities of the world their discipline has preserved them, and the English character owes to their example some part of its manly plainness in externals. But my argument is confined to the question, whether Religion in its present state and under the present conceptions of its demands and purposes does, even among the most religious, exert any efficient force of controul over the commercial spirit, the excess of which we have attributed not to the extent and magnitude of the commerce itself, but to the absence or imperfection of its appointed checks and counteragents. Now as the system of the Friends in its first intention is of all others most hostile to worldly-mindedness on the one hand; and as, on the other, the adherents of this system both in confession and *practice* confine Christianity to feelings and motives; they may be selected as representatives of the strict, but unstudied and un-inquiring, Religionists of every denomination. Their characteristic propensities will supply, therefore, no unfair test for the degree of resistance, which our present Christianity is capable of opposing to the cupidity of a trading people. That species of Christianity I mean, which, as far as knowledge and the faculties of thought are concerned,—which, as far as the growth and grandeur of the *intellectual* man is in question—is to be learnt ex tempore! A Christianity poured in on the Catechumen all and all at once, as from a shower-bath: and which, whatever it may be in the heart, yet for the understanding and reason is from boyhood onward a thing past and perfected! If the almost universal opinion be tolerably correct, the question is answered. But I by no means *appropriate* the remark to the wealthy Quakers, or even apply it to them in any particular or eminent sense, when I say, that often as the motely reflexes of my experience move in long procession of manifold groups before me, the distinguished and world-honored company of Christian Mammonists appear to the eye of my imagination as a drove of camels heavily laden, yet all at full speed, and each in the confident expectation of passing through the EYE OF THE NEEDLE, without stop or halt, both beasts and baggage.

Not without an uneasy reluctance have I ventured to tell the truth on this subject, least I should be charged with the indulgence of a satirical mood and an uncharitable spleen. But my conscience bears me witness, and I know myself too near the grave to trifle with its name, that I am solely actuated by a sense of the *exceeding* importance of the subject at the present moment. I feel it an awful duty to exercise the honest liberty of free utterance in so dear a concernment as that of preparing my country for a change in its external relations, which must come sooner or later; which I believe to have already commenced; and that it will depend on the presence or absence of a corresponding change in the *mind* of the nation, and above all in the aims and ruling opinions of our gentry and moneyed men, whether it is to cast down our strength and prosperity, or to fix them on a firmer and more august basis. "Surely to every good and peaceable man it must in nature needs be a hateful thing to be the displeaser and molester of thousands; but when God commands to take the trumpet and blow a dolorous or a jarring blast, it lies not in man's will what he shall say and what he shall conceal."

That my complaints, both in this and in my former Lay Sermon, concerning the same errors, are not grounded on any peculiar notions of mine, the following remarks of a great and good man, not less illustrious for his piety and fervent zeal as a Christian than for his acuteness and profundity as a Philosopher, may, perhaps, be accepted as proof.

"Prevailing studies, he observes, are of no

small consequence to a state, the religion, manners, and civil government of a country ever taking some bias from its philosophy, which affects not only the minds of its professors and students, but also the opinions of all the better sort, and the practice of the whole people, remotely and consequentially indeed, though not inconsiderably. Have not the doctrines of Necessity and Materialism, with the consequent denial of men's responsibility, of his corrupt and fallen nature, and of the whole scheme of Redemption by the incarnate Word gained ground during the general passion for the Corpuscularian and Experimental Philosophy which hath prevailed about a century? This indeed might usefully enough have employed some share of the leisure and curiosity of inquisitive persons. But when it entered the seminaries of Learning, as a necessary accomplishment and as the most important part of knowledge, by engrossing men's thoughts and fixing their minds so much on corporeal objects, it hath, however undesignedly, not a little indisposed them for spiritual, moral, and intellectual matters. Certainly, had the philosophy of Pythagoras and Socrates prevailed in this age, we should not have seen interest take so general and fast hold on the minds of men. But while the employment of the mind on things purely intellectual is to most men irksome, whereas the sensitive powers by our constant use of them, acquire strength, the objects of sense are too often counted the chief good. For these things men fight, cheat, and scramble. Therefore, in order to tame mankind and introduce a sense of virtue, *the best human means is to exercise their understanding*, to give them a glimpse of a world superior to the sensible: and while they take pains to cherish and maintain the animal life, to teach them not to neglect the intellectual.

It might very well be thought serious trifling to tell my readers that the greatest men had ever an high esteem for Plato; whose writings are the touchstone of an hasty and shallow mind; whose philosophy, the admiration of ages, supplied patriots, magistrates and lawgivers to the most flourishing states, as well fathers to the Church, and doctors to the Schools. In these days the depths of that old learning are rarely fathomed: and yet it were happy for these lands, if our young nobility and *gentry instead of modern maxims would imbibe the notions of the great men of antiquity.* But in these free-thinking times, many an empty head is shook at Aristotle and Plato: and the writings of these celebrated ancients are by most men treated on a level with the dry and barbarous lucubrations of the Schoolmen. It may, however, be modestly presumed that there are not many among us, even of those that are called the better sort, who have more sense, virtue, and love of their country than Cicero, who in a letter to Atticus could not forbear exclaiming, O Socrates et Socratici Viri! nunquam vobis gratiam referam. Would to God, many of our countrymen had the same obligations to those Socratic writers. Certainly, where the people are well educated, the art of piloting a state is best learnt from the writings of Plato. But among a people void of discipline a gentry devoted to vulgar cares and views, Plato, Pythagoras, and Aristotle themselves, were they living, could do but little good."

Thus then, of the three most approved antagonists to the Spirit of Barter, and the accompanying disposition to overvalue Riches with all the Means and tokens thereof—of the three fittest and most likely checks to this tendency, namely, the feeling of ancient birth and the respect paid to it by the community at large; a genuine intellectual Philosophy with an accredited, learned, and Philosophic *Class;* and lastly, Religion; we have found the first declining, the second not existing, and the third efficient, indeed, in many respects and to many excellent purposes, only not in this particular direction: the Religion here spoken of, having long since parted company with that inquisitive and bookish Theology which tends to defraud the student of his worldly wisdom, inasmuch as it diverts his mind from the accumulation of wealth by pre-occupying his thoughts in the acquisition of knowledge. For the Religion of best repute among us holds all the truths of Scripture and all the doctrines of Christianity so very transcendent, or so very easy, as to make study and research either vain or needless. It professes, therefore, to hunger and thirst after Righteousness alone, and the rewards of the Righteous; and thus habitually *taking for granted* all truths of spiritual import leaves the understanding vacant and at leisure for a thorough insight into present and temporal interests: which, doubtless, is the true reason why its followers, are in general such shrewd, knowing, wary, well-informed, thrifty and thriving men of business. But this is likewise the reason, why it neither does or can check or circumscribe the Spirit of Barter; and to the consequent *monopoly* which this commercial Spirit possesses, must its over-balance be attributed, not to the extent or magnitude of the Commerce itself.

Before I enter on the result assigned by me as the chief ultimate *cause* of the present state of the country, and as the main *ground* on which the immediate occasions of the general distress have worked, I must entreat my Readers to reflect that the spirit of Trade has been a thing of insensible growth; that whether it be enough, or more or less than enough, is a matter of relative, rather than of positive determination; that it depends on the degree in which it is aided or resisted by all the other tendencies that co-exist with it; and that in the best of times this spirit may be said to live on a narrow isthmus between a sterile desert and a stormy sea, still threatened and encroached on either by the Too Much or Too Little. As the argument does not depend on any precise accuracy in the dates, I shall assume it to have commenced, as an influencing part of the national character, with the institution of the Funds in the reign of William the Third, and from the peace of Aix-la-Chapelle in 1748, to have been hurrying onward to its maximum, which it seems to have attained during the late war. The short interruptions may be well represented as a few steps backward, that it might leap forward with an additional momentum. The words, old and modern, now and then, are applied by me, the latter to the whole period since the Revolution, and the former to the interval between this epoch and the Reformation; the one from 1460 to 1680, the other from 1680 to the present time.

Having premised this explanation, I can now return an intelligible answer to a question, that will have risen in the Reader's mind during his perusal of the last three or four pages. How, it will be objected, does all this apply to the present times in particular? When was the industrious part of mankind *not* attached to the pursuits most likely to reward their industry?

Was the wish to make a fortune or, if you prefer an invidious phrase, the lust of lucre, less natural to our forefathers than to their descendants? If you say, that though a not less frequent, or less powerful passion with them than with us, it yet met with a more frequent and more powerful check, a stronger and more advanced boundary-line, in the Religion of old times, and in the faith, fashion, habits, and authority of the Religious: in what did this difference consist? and in what way did these points of difference act? If indeed the antidote in question once possessed virtues which it no longer possesses, or not in the same degree, what is the ingredient, either added, omitted, or diminished since that time, which can have rendered it less efficacious now than then?

Well! (I might reply) grant all this: and let both the profession and the professors of a spiritual principle, as a counterpoise to the worldly weights at the other end of the Balance, be supposed much the same in the one period as in the other! Assume for a moment, that I can establish neither the fact of its lesser efficiency, nor any points of difference capable of accounting for it! Yet it might still be a sufficient answer to this objection, that as the commerce of the country, and with it the spirit of commerce, has increased fifty-fold since the commencement of the latter period, it is not enough that the counterweight should be as great as it was in the former period: to remain the same in its effect, it ought to have become very much greater. But though this be a consideration not less important than it is obvious, yet I do not purpose to rest in it. I affirm, that a difference may be shewn, and of no trifling importance as to that one point, to which my present argument is confined. For let it be remembered, that it is not to any extraordinary influences of the religious principle that I am referring, not to voluntary poverty, or sequestration from social and active life, or schemes of mortification. I speak of Religion merely as I should of any worldly object, which, as far as it employs and interests a man, leaves less room in his mind for other pursuits: except that this must be more especially the case in the instance of Religion because beyond all other Interests it is calculated to occupy the whole mind, and employ successively all the faculties of man: and because the objects which it presents to the Imagination as well as to the Intellect cannot be actually contemplated, much less can they be the subject of frequent meditation, without dimming the lustre and blunting the rays of all rival attractions. It is well known, and has been observed of old, that Poetry tends to render its devotees* careless of money and outward appearances, while Philosophy inspires a contempt of both as objects of Desire or Admiration. But Religion is the Poetry and Philosophy of all mankind; unites in itself whatever is most excellent in either, and while it at one and the same time calls into action and supplies with the noblest materials both the imaginative and the intellective faculties, superadds the interests of the most substantial and home-felt reality to both, to the poetic vision and the philosophic idea. But in order to

---

* Hic error tamen et levis hic insania quantas
Virtutes habeat, sic collige: vatis avarus
Non temere est animus; versus amat, hoc studet unum;
Detrimenta, fugas servorum, incendia ridet;
Non fraudem socio, puerove incogitat ullam
Pupillo; vivit siliquis et pane secundo:
Militiæ quanquam piger et malus, utilis urbi.

HORAT. EPIST. II. 1.

produce a similar effect it must act in a similar way: it must reign in the thoughts of a man and in the powers akin to thought, as well as exercise an admitted influence over his hopes and fears, and through these on his deliberate and individual acts.

Now as my first presumptive proof of a difference (I might almost have said, of a contrast) between the religious character of the period since the Revolution, and that of the period from the accession of Edward the Sixth to the abdication of the second James, I refer to the Sermons and to the theological Works generally, of the latter period. It is my full conviction, that in any half dozen Sermons of Dr. Donne, or Jeremy Taylor, there are more thoughts, more facts and images, more excitements to inquiry and intellectual effort, than are presented to the congregations of the present day in as many churches or meetings during twice as many months. Yet both these were the most popular preachers of their times, were heard with enthusiasm by crowded and promiscuous Audiences, and the effect produced by their eloquence was held in reverential and affectionate remembrance by many attendants on their ministry, who like the pious Isaac Walton, were not themselves men of learning or education. In addition to this fact, think likewise on the large and numerous editions of massy, closely printed folios: the impressions so large and the editions so numerous, that all the industry of destruction for the last hundred years has but of late sufficed to make them rare. From the long list select those works alone, which we know to have been the most current and favorite works of their day: and of these again no more than may well be supposed to have had a place in the scantiest libraries, or perhaps with the Bible and Common Prayer Book to have *formed* the library of their owner. Yet on the single shelf so filled we should find almost every possible question, that could interest or instruct a reader whose whole heart was in his religion, discussed with a command of intellect that seems to exhaust all the learning and logic, all the historical and moral relations, of each several subject. The very length of the discourses, with which these "rich souls of wit and knowledge" fixed the eyes, ears, and hearts of their crowded congregations, are a source of wonder now-a-days, and (we may add,) of self-congratulation, to many a sober christian, who forgets with what delight he himself has listened to a two hours' harangue on a Loan or Tax, or at the trial of some remarkable cause or culprit. The transfer of the interest makes and explains the whole difference. For though much may be fairly charged on the revolution in the *mode* of preaching as well as in the matter, since the fresh morning and fervent noon of the Reformation, when there was no need to visit the conventicles of fanaticism in order to

>See God's ambassador in the pulpit stand,
>Where they could take notes from his Look and Hand;
>And from his speaking *action* bear away
>More sermon than our preachers use to *say;*

yet this too must be referred to the same change in the habits of men's minds, a change that involves both the shepherd and the flock: though like many other *Effects*, it tends to reproduce and strengthen its own cause.

The last point, to which I shall appeal, is the warmth and frequency of the religious controversies during the former of the two periods; the deep interest excited by them among all but the lowest and most ignorant classes; the importance attached to them by the very highest; the number, and in many instances the transcendent merit, of the controversial publications—in short, the rank and value assigned to *polemic divinity*. The subjects of the controversies may or may not have been trifling; the warmth, with which they were conducted, may have been disproportionate and indecorous; and we may have reason to congratulate ourselves that the age, in which we live, is grown more indulgent and less captious. The fact is introduced not for its own sake, but as a *symptom* of the general state of men's feelings, as an evidence of the direction and main channel, in which the thoughts and interests of men were then flowing. We all know, that lovers are apt to take offence and wrangle with each other on occasions that perhaps are but trifles, and which assuredly would appear such to those who had never been under the influence of a similar passion. These quarrels may be no proofs of wisdom; but still in the imperfect state of our nature the entire absence of the same, and this too on far more serious provocations, would excite a strong suspicion of a comparative *indifference* in the feelings of the parties towards each other, who can love so coolly where they profess to love so well. I shall believe our present religious tolerancy to proceed from the abundance of our charity and good sense, when I can see proofs that we are equally cool and forbearing, as Litigators and political Partizans. And I must again intreat my reader to recollect, that the present argument is exclusively concerned with the requisite correctives of the commercial spirit, and with Religion therefore no otherwise, than as a counter-charm to the sorcery of wealth: and my main position is that neither by reasons drawn from the nature of the human mind, or by facts of actual experience, are we justified in expecting this from a religion which does not employ and actuate the understandings of men, and combine their affections with it as a system of Truth gradually and progressively manifesting itself to the intellect; no less than as a system of motives and moral commands learnt as soon as heard, and containing nothing but what is plain and easy to the lowest capacities. Hence it is, that Objects, the ostensible principle of which I have felt it my duty to oppose (vide the STATESMAN's MANUAL, p. 54.) and objects, the which and the measures for the attainment of which possess my good wishes and have had the humble tribute of my public advocation and applause—I am here alluding to the British and Foreign Bible Society—may yet converge, as to the point now in question. They may, both alike, be symptoms of the same predominant disposition to that Coalition-system in Christianity, for the expression of which Theologians have invented or appropriated the term, *Syncretism:** although the former may be an ominous, the latter an auspicious

---

* Clementia Evangelica (writes a German Theologian of the last Century) quasi matrona habenda est, purioris doctrinæ custos, mitis quidem, at sedula tamen, at vigilans, at seductorum impatiens. Iste vero Syncretismus, quem Laodiceni apud nos tantopere collaudant, nusquam a me nisi meretrix audiet, Fidei vel pigræ vel status sui ignaræ proles, postea autem indolis secularis genetrix, et quâcum nec sincera fides, nec genuina Caritas commorari feret.

Translation.—The true Gospel Spirit of Toleration we should regard as a Matron, a kind and gentle guardian indeed of the pure Doctrine, but sedulous, but vigilant, but impatient of Seducers. This SYNCRETISM on the contrary, which the Loadiceans among us join in extolling so highly, shall no where

symptom, though the one may be worse from Bad, while the other is an instance of Good educed from Evil. Nay, I will dare confess, that I know not how to think otherwise, when I hear a Bishop of an established Church publicly exclaim (and not viewing it as a lesser inconvenience to be endured for the attainment of a far greater good, but as a thing desirable and to be preferred for its own sake) *No Notes! No Comment! Distribute the Bible and the Bible only among the Poor!*—a declaration, which from any lower quarter I should have been under the temptation of attributing either to a fanatical notion of immediate illumination superseding the necessity of human teaching, or to an ignorance of difficulties which (and what more worthy?) have *successfully* employed all the learning, sagacity, and unwearied labors of great and wise men, and eminent servants of Christ, during all the ages of Christianity, and will doubtless continue to yield

hear from me other or better name than that of Harlot, the offspring of a Belief either slothful or ignorant of its own condition, and then the parent of Worldly-mindedness, and with whom therefore neither sincere Faith nor genuine Charity will endure to associate.

new fruits of Knowledge and Insight to a long series of Followers.*

Though an overbalance of the commercial spirit is involved in the deficiency of its counterweights; yet the facts, that exemplify the mode and extent of its operation, will afford a more direct and satisfactory kind of proof. And first I am to speak of this overbalance as displayed in the commercial world itself. But as this is the first, so is it for my present

* I am well aware, that by these open avowals, that with much to honor and praise in many, there is something to correct in all, parties, I shall provoke many enemies and make never a friend. If I *dared* abstain, how gladly should I have so done! Would that the candid part of my Judges would peruse or re-peruse the affecting and most eloquent introductory pages of Milton's Second Book of his " Reason of Church Government urged, &c. ;" and give me the credit, which (my conscience bears me witness) I am entitled to claim, for all the *moral* feelings expressed in that exquisite passage. The following paragraph I extract from a volume of my own, which has been long printed, for the greater part, and which will, I trust, now be soon published.

" All my experience from my first entrance into life to the present hour is in favour of the warning maxim, that the man who opposes in toto the political or religious zealots of his age, is safer from their obloquy than he who differs from them in any one or two points or perhaps only in degree. By that transfer of the feelings of private life into the discussions of public questions, which is the *queen bee* in the hive of party

purpose the least important point of view. A portion of the facts belonging to this division, of the subject I have already noticed, p. 37. 38; and for the remainder let the following suffice as the substitute or representative. The moral of the tale I leave to the Reader's own reflections. Within the last sixty years or perhaps a somewhat larger period, (for I do not pretend to any nicety of dates, and the documents are of easy access) there have occurred at intervals of about 12 or 13 years

fanaticism, the partizan has more sympathy with an intemperate opposite than with a moderate Friend. We now enjoy an intermission and long may it continue! In addition to far higher and more important merits, our present bible societies, and other numerous associations for national or charitable objects, may serve perhaps to carry off the superfluous activity and fervor of stirring minds in innocent hyperboles and the bustle of management. But the poison-tree is not dead, though the sap may for a season have subsided to its roots. At least, let us not be lulled into such a notion of our entire security, as not to keep watch and ward, even on our best feelings. I have seen gross intolerance shewn in support of toleration; sectarian antipathy most obtrusively displayed in the promotion of an undistinguishing comprehension of sects; and acts of cruelty (I had almost said) of treachery, committed in furtherance of an object vitally important to the cause of humanity; and all this by men too of naturally kind dispositions and exemplary conduct."—*Biographia Literaria, or Sketches of my Literary Life, and Opinions*, p. 190.

each, certain periodical Revolutions of Credit. Yet Revolution is not the precise word. To state the thing as it is, I ought to have said, certain gradual expansions of credit ending in sudden contractions, or, with equal propriety, ascensions to a certain utmost possible height, which has been different in each successive instance; but in every instance the attainment of this, its ne plus ultra, has been instantly announced by a rapid series of explosions (in mercantile language, a *Crash*) and a consequent precipitation of the general system. For a short time this Icarian* Credit, or rather this illegitimate offspring of CONFIDENCE, to which it stands in the same relation as Phaethon to his parent god in the old fable, seems to lie stunned by the fall; but soon re-

---

* "Icarus, Son of Dædalus, who flying with his father from Crete flew too high, whereby the sun melting his waxen wings he fell into the Sea, from him named the Icarian Sea."—AINSWORTH. By turning back to the word Dædalus, the Reader will find such a striking and ingenious allegory of the Manufacturing System, its connections with a forced or contraband Trade, and its succesful evasions of what has been lately called the *continental system*, as may induce him to forgive the triteness and school-boy character which all allusions of this sort have at first sight for a sensible mind.

covering, again it strives upward, and having once more regained its mid region,

> ——— thence many a league,
> As in a cloudy chair, ascending rides
> Audacious!
>
> PARADISE LOST.

till at the destined zenith of its vaporous exaltation, "*all unawares, fluttering its pennons vain, plumb down it drops!*" Or that I may descend myself to the "cool element of prose," Alarm and suspicion gradually diminish into a judicious circumspectness; but by little and little, circumspection gives way to the desire and emulous ambition of *doing business*: till Impatience and Incaution on one side, tempting and encouraging headlong Adventure, Want of principle, and Confederacies of false credit on the other, the movements of Trade become yearly gayer and giddier, and end at length in a vortex of hopes and hazards, of blinding passions and blind practices, which should have been left where alone they ought ever to have been found, among the wicked lunacies of the Gaming Table.

I am not ignorant that the power and circumstantial prosperity of the Nation has been increasing during the same period, with an accelerated force unprecedented in any country, the population of which bore the same proportion to its productive soil: and partly, perhaps, even in consequence of this system. By facilitating the *means* of enterprize it must have called into activity a multitude of enterprizing Individuals and a variety of Talent that would otherwise have lain dormant: while by the same ready supply of excitements to Labor, together with its materials and instruments, even an unsound credit has been able within a short time to* substantiate itself. We shall

* If by the display of forged Bank Notes a Speculator should establish the belief of his being a Man of large fortune, and gain a temporary confidence in his own paper-money; and if by large wages so paid he should stimulate a number of indolent Highlanders to bring a tract of waste land into profitable cultivation, the promissory Notes of the Owner, which derived their first value from a delusion, would end in representing a real property, and this their own product. A most improbable case! In its accidental features, I reply, rather than in its essentials. How many thousand acres have been reclaimed from utter unproductiveness, how many doubled in value, by the agency of notes issued beyond the bonâ fide Capital of the Bank or Firm that circulated them, or at best on Capital afloat and insecure.

In this section of the present address, I consider myself as

perhaps be told too, that the very Evils of this System, even the periodical *crash* itself, are to be regarded but as so much superfluous steam ejected by the Escape Pipes and Safety Valves of a self-regulating Machine: and lastly, that in a free and trading country *all things find their level.*

I have as little disposition as motive to recant the principles, which in many forms and through various channels I have labored to propagate; but there is surely no inconsistency in yielding all due honor to the spirit of Trade, and yet charging sundry evils, that weaken or reverse its blessings, on the over-balance of that spirit, taken as the paramount principle of action in the Nation at large. Much I still concede to the arguments for the present scheme of Things, as adduced in the preceding paragraph: but I likewise see, and always have seen, much that needs winnowing. Thus instead of the po-

having redeemed a promise, made by me (November 1809) in the Essay "On vulgar errors concerning Taxation." Having demonstrated the favourable influences of the system "on our political strength and *circumstantial* prosperity," THE FRIEND added the following pledge: "What have been the *injurious* effects on our Literature, Morals, and Religious Principles, I shall hereafter develope with the same boldness,"

tion, that all things *find*, it would be less equivocal and far more descriptive of the fact to say, that things are always *finding*, their level: which might be taken as the paraphrase or ironical definition of a storm, but would be still more appropriate to the Mosaic Chaos, ere its brute tendencies had been enlightened by the WORD (i. e. the communicative Intelligence) and before the Spirit of Wisdom* moved on the *level-finding* Waters. But Persons are not *Things*—but man does not find his level. Neither in body nor in soul does the Man find his level! After a hard and calamitous season, during which the thousand Wheels of some vast manufactory had remained silent as a frozen water-fall, be it that plenty has returned and that Trade has once more become brisk and stirring: go, ask the overseer, and question the parish doctor, whether the workman's health and temperance with the staid and respectful Manners best taught by the inward dignity of conscious self-support,

* Σοφία, Wisdom, (that is, Reason in Act or Energy) was the name by which the Christians and Christian Writers of the three first Centuries most commonly addressed and distinguished the Holy Ghost.

have found *their* level again! Alas! I have more than once seen a group of children in Dorsetshire, during the heat of the dog-days, each with its little shoulders up to its ears, and its chest pinched inward, the very habit and *fixtures*, as it were, that had been impressed on their frames by the former ill-fed, ill-clothed, and unfuelled winters. But as with the Body, so or still worse with the Mind. Nor is the effect confined to the laboring classes, whom by an ominous but too appropriate a change in our phraseology we are now accustomed to call the Laboring Poor. I cannot persuade myself, that the frequency of Failures with all the disgraceful secrets of Fraud and Folly, of unprincipled Vanity in expending and desperate Speculation in retrieving, can be familiarized to the thoughts and experience of Men, as matters of daily occurrence, without serious injury to the Moral Sense: more especially in times when Bankruptcies spread, like a fever, at once contagious and epidemic; swift too as the travel of an Earthquake, that with one and the same chain of Shocks opens the ruinous chasm in cities that have an ocean between them!—in times, when the Fate flies swifter than the Fear, and yet the report, that follows the flash, has a ruin of its own and arrives but to multiply the Blow!—when princely capitals are often but the Telegraphs of distant calamity: and still worse, when no man's treasure is safe who has adopted the ordinary means of safety, neither the high or the humble; when the Lord's rents and the Farmer's store, entrusted perhaps but as yesterday, are asked after at closed doors!—but worst of all, in its moral influences as well as in the cruelty of suffering, when the old Laborers' Savings, the precious robberies of self-denial from every day's comfort; when the Orphan's Funds; the Widow's Livelihood; the fond confiding Sister's humble Fortune; are found among the victims to the remorseless mania of dishonest Speculation, or to the desperate cowardice of Embarrassment, and the drunken stupor of a usurious Selfishness that for a few months respite dares incur a debt of guilt and infamy, for which the grave itself can plead no statute of limitation. Name to me any Revolution recorded in History, that was not followed by a depravation of the national Morals. The Roman character during the Triumvirate, and under Tiberius; the reign of Charles the Second; and Paris at the present moment; are obvious instances. What is the main cause? The sense of Insecurity. On what ground then dare we hope, that with the same accompaniment Commercial Revolutions should not produce the same effect, in proportion to the extent of their sphere?

But these Blessings—with all the specific terms, into which this most comprehensive Phrase is to be resolved? Dare we unpack the bales and cases so marked, and look at the articles, one by one? Increase of human Life and increase of the means of Life are, it is true, reciprocally cause and effect: and the Genius of Commerce and Manufactory has been the cause of both to a degree that may well excite our *wonder*. But do the last results justify our exultation likewise? Human Life, alas! is but the malleable Metal, out of which the thievish Picklock, the Slave's Collar, and the Assassin's Stiletto are formed as well as the clearing Axe, the feeding Plough-share, the defensive Sword, and the mechanic Tool. But the subject is a painful one: and fortunately the labors of others, with the communications of medical men concerning the state of the manufacturing Poor, have rendered it unnecessary. I will rather (though in strict method it should, perhaps, be reserved for the following Head) relate a speech made to me near Fort Augustus, as I was travelling on foot through the Highlands of Scotland. The Speaker was an elderly and respectable widow, who expressed herself with that simple eloquence, which strong feeling seldom fails to call forth in humble life, but especially in women. She spoke English, as indeed most Highlanders do who speak it all, with a propriety of phrase and a discrimination of tone and emphasis that more than compensated for the scantiness of her vocabulary. After an affecting account of her own wrongs and ejectment, (which however, she said, bore with comparative lightness on her, who had had saved up for her a wherewithal to live, and was blessed with a son well to do in the world), she made a movement with her hand in a circle, directing my eye meanwhile to various objects as marking its outline: and then observed, with a deep sigh and a suppressed and slow voice which she suddenly raised and quickened after the first drop or cadence—Within this space—how short a time back! there lived a hundred and seventy-three persons: and now there is only a shepherd, and an underling or two. Yes, Sir! One hundred and seventy-three Christian souls, man, woman, boy, girl, and babe; and in almost every home an old man by the fire-side, who would tell you of the troubles, before our roads were made; and many a brave youth among them who loved the birth-place of his forefathers, yet would swing about his broad-sword and want but a word to march off to the battles over sea; aye Sir, and many a good lass, who had a respect for herself! Well! but they are gone, and with them the bristled bear,* and the pink haver,† and the potatoe plot that looked as gay as any flower garden with its blossoms! I sometimes fancy, that the very birds are gone, all but the crows and the gleads! Well, and what then? Instead of us all, there is one shepherd man, and it may be a pair of small lads—and a many, many sheep! And do you think, Sir! that God allows of such proceedings?

Some days before this conversation, and

* A species of Barley. † A species of Oats.

while I was on the shores of the Loch Kathern,* I had heard of a sad counterpart to the widow's tale, and told with a far fiercer indignation, of a " Laird who had raised a company from the country round about, for the love that was borne to his name, and who gained high preferment in consequence: and that it was but a small part of those that he took away whom he brought back again. And what were the thanks which the folks had both for those that came back with him, some blind and more in danger of blindness; and for those that had perished in the hospitals, and for those that fell in battle, fighting before or beside him? Why, that their fathers were all turned out of their farms before the year was over, and sent to wander like so many gipsies, unless they would consent to shed their gray hairs, at tenpence a day, over the new canals. Had there

* The Lake so widely celebrated since then by a Poet, to whose writings a larger number of persons have owed a larger portion of innocent, and heart-bettering amusement, than perhaps to any favorite of the Muses recorded in English literature: while the most learned of his readers must feel grateful for the mass of interesting and highly instructive information scattered throughout his works, in which respect Southey is his only rival.

been a price set upon his head, and his enemies had been coming upon him, he needed but have whistled, and a hundred brave lads would have made a wall of flame round about him with the flash of their broad-swords! Now if the———should come among us, as (it is said)they will, let him whistle to his sheep and see if *they* will fight for him!" The frequency with which I heard, during my solitary walk from the end of Loch-Lomond to Inverness, confident expectations of the kind expressed in his concluding words—nay, far too often eager hopes mingled with vindictive resolves— I spoke of with complaint and regret to an elderly man: whom by his dress and way of speaking, I took to be a schoolmaster. Long shall I recollect his reply: "O, Sir, it kills a man's love for his country, the hardships of life coming by change and with injustice!" I was sometime afterwards told by a very sensible person who had studied the mysteries of political œconomy, and was therefore entitled to be listened to, that more food was produced in consequence of this revolution, that the mutton must be eat somewhere, and what difference where? If three were fed at Manchester instead of two at Glenco or the Trossacs, the balance of human enjoyment was, in favor of the former. I have passed through many a manufacturing town since then, and watched many a group of old and young, male and female, going to, or returning from, many a factory, but I could never yet persuade myself to be of his opinion. Men, I still think, ought to be weighed not counted. Their *worth* ought to be the final estimate of their value.

Among the occasions and minor causes of this change in the views and measures of our Land-owners, and as being itself a consequent on that system of credit, the outline of which was given in a preceding page, the universal practice of enhancing the sale price of every article on the presumption of Bad Debts, is not the least noticeable. Nor, if we reflect that this additional per centage is repeated at each intermediate stage of its elaboration and distribution from the Grower or Importer to the last Retailer *inclusively*, will it appear the least operative. Necessary, and therefore justifiable, as this plan of reprisal by anticipation may be in the case of each individual dealer, yet taken collectively and without reference to persons, the plan itself would, I suspect, startle an unfamiliarized conscience, as a sort of nondescript Piracy, not promiscuous in its exactions only because by a curious anomaly it grants a free pass to the offending party. Or if the Law maxim, *volentibus nulla fit injuria*, is applicable in this case, it may perhaps be described more courteously as a *Benefit Society* of all the careful and honest men in the kingdom to pay the debts of the dishonest or improvident. It is mentioned here, however, as one of the appendages to the twin paramount causes, the Paper Currency and the National Debt, and for the sake of the conjoint results. Would we learn what these results are? What they have been in the higher, and what in the most numerous, class of society? Alas! that some of the intermediate rounds in the social ladder have been broken and not replaced, is itself one of these results. Retrace the progress of things from 1792 to 1813, when the tide was at its height, and then, as far as its rapidity will permit, the ebb from its first turn to the dead low-water mark of the last quarter. Then see whether the remainder may not be generalized under the following heads. Fluctuation in the wages of labor, alternate privation and excess (not in all at the same time, but successively in each) consequent improvidence, and over all discontent and a system of factious confederacy—these form the history of the mechanics and lower ranks of our cities and towns. In the country, a peasantry sinking into pauperism, step for step with the rise of the farmer's profits and indulgencies. On the side of the landlord and his compeers, we shall find the presence of the same causes attested by answerable effects. Great as "their almost magical effects" * on the increase of prices were in the necessaries of life, they

* During the composition of this sheet I have had, and availed myself of the opportunity of perusing the Report of the Board of Agriculture for the year 1816. The numerous reflections, which this most extraordinary volume excited in my mind, I cannot even touch on, in this closing sheet of an Address that has already extended far beyond my original purpose. But had I perused it at the commencement, I should still have felt it my duty to direct the main force of my animadversions against the Demagogue class of State empirics. I was not indeed, ignorant of the aid, which they derived from other quarters:—nor am I now ashamed of not having anticipated its extent. There is, however, one communication (p. 208 to 227) from Mr. Mosely, from which, with the abate-

were still greater, disproportionally greater, in all articles of shew and luxury. With few exceptions, it soon became difficult, and at length impracticable, for the gentry of the land, for the possessors of fixed property to retain the rank of their ancestors, or their own former establishments, without joining in the general competition under the influence of the same trading spirit. Their dependants were of course either selected from, or driven into, the same eddy; while the temptation of obtaining more than the legal interest for their principal became more and more strong with all persons who, neither trading nor farming, had lived on the interest of their fortunes. It was in this latter class that the rash, and too frequently, the unprincipled projector found his readiest dupes. Had we but the secret history of the *building* speculations only in the vicinity of the metropolis, too many of its pages would supply an afflicting but instructive comment. That both here, and in all other departments, this increased momentum in the spirit of trade

ment only of the passage on tythes, I cannot withhold my entire admiration. It almost redeems the remainder of the Report.

has been followed by results of the most desirable nature, I have myself*, exerted my best powers to evince, at a period when to present the fairest and most animating features of the system, and to prove their vast and charm-like influence on the power and resources of the nation appeared a duty of patriotism. Nothing, however, was advanced incompatible with the position, which even then I did not conceal, and which from the same sense of duty I am now attempting to display; namely, that the extension of the commercial spirit into our agricultural system, *added* to the overbalance of the same spirit, even within its own sphere; *aggravated* by the operation of our Revenue Laws; and finally *reflected* in the habits, and tendencies of the Laboring Classes; is the ground-work of our calamity, and the main

---

* In a variety of articles published at different periods in the Morning Post and Courier; but with most success in the Essay, before cited, on Vulgar Errors on Taxation, which had the advantage of being transferred almost entire to the columns of a daily paper, of the largest circulation, and from thence, in larger or smaller extracts, to several of our Provincial Journals. It was likewise reprinted in two of the American Federalist Papers: and a translation appeared, I have been told, in the Hamburgh Correspondenten.

predisposing cause, without which the late *occasions* would (some of them not have existed, and the remainder) not have produced the present distresses.

That Agriculture requires principles essentially different from those of Trade,—that a gentleman ought not to regard his estate as a merchant his cargo, or a shopkeeper his stock,—admits of an easy proof from the different tenure of Landed Property,* and from the purposes of Agriculture itself, which ultimately are

* The very idea of *individual* or private property, in our present acceptation of the term, and according to the current notion of the *right* to it, was originally confined to moveable things: and the more moveable, the more susceptible of the nature of property. Proceeding from the more to the less perfect *right;* we may bring all the objects of an independent ownership under five heads:—viz. 1. Precious stones, and other jewels of as easy transfer; 2. The precious metals, and foreign coin taken as weight of metal; 3. Merchandize, by virtue of the contract between the importer and the sovereign in whose person the unity and integrity of the *common* wealth were represented; i. e. after the settled price had been paid by the former for the permission to import, and received by the latter under the further obligation of protecting the same; 4. The coin of the Country in the possession of the natural subject; and last of all, and in *certain* cases, the live stock, the *peculium a pecus*. Hence, the minds of men were most familiar with the idea in the case of Jews and Aliens; till gradually, the privileges attached to the vicinity of the Bishops and mitred

the same as those of the State of which it is the offspring. (For we do not include in the name of Agriculture the cultivation of a few vegetables by the women of the less savage Hunter Tribes.) If the continuance and independence of the State be its object, the final causes of the State must be its final causes. We suppose the negative ends of a State already attained, viz. its own safety by means of its own strength, and the protection of person and property for all its members, there will then remain its positive ends:—1. To make the means of subsistence more easy to each individual. 2. To secure to each of its members THE HOPE* of bettering his own condition or that of his children. 3. The develope-

---

Abbots prepared an asylum for the fugitive Vassal and the oppressed Frankling, and thus laid the first foundations of a fourth class of freemen, that of Citizens and Burghers. To the Feudal system we owe the *forms*, to the Church the *substance* of our liberty. As comment take, first, the origin of towns and cities; next the holy war waged against slavery and villenage, and with such success that the law had barely to sanction an opus jam consum

[This note is left imperfect in the London copy. Am. Pub.]

* The Civilized man gives up those stimulants of Hope and Fear, the mixture or alternation of which constitutes the chief charm of the savage life: and yet his Maker has distinguished

ment of those faculties which are essential to his Humanity, i. e. to his rational and moral Being. Under the last head we do not mean those degrees of intellectual cultivation which distinguish man from man in the same civilized society, but those only that raise the civilized man above the Barbarian, the Savage, and the Animal. We require, however, on the part of the State, in behalf of all its members, not only the outward means of *knowing* their essential duties and dignities as men and free men, but likewise, and more especially, the discouragement of all such Tenures and Relations as must in the very nature of things render this knowledge inert, and cause the good seed to perish as it falls. Such at least is the appointed Aim of a State: and at whatever distance from the ideal Mark the existing circumstances of a nation may unhappily place the actual statesman,.

him from the Brute that perishes, by making Hope an instinct of his nature and an indispensable condition of his moral and intellectual progression. But a natural instinct constitutes a natural right, as far as its gratification is compatible with the equal rights of others. Hence our ancestors classed those who were incapable of altering their condition from that of their parents, as Bondsmen or Villains, however advantageously they might otherwise be situated.

still every movement ought to be in this direction. But the negative merit of not forwarding —but the exemption from the crime of necessitating—the debasement and virtual disfranchisement of any class of the community, may be demanded of every State under all circumstances: and the Government, that pleads difficulties in repulse or demur of this claim, impeaches its own wisdom and fortitude. But as the *specific* ends of Agriculture are the maintenance, strength, and security of the State, so (we repeat) must its *ultimate* ends be the same as those of the State: even as the ultimate end of the spring and wheels of a watch must be the same as that of the watch. Yet least of all things dare we overlook or conceal, that morally and with respect to the character and conscience of the Individuals, the Blame of unfaithful Stewardship is aggravated, in proportion as the Difficulties are less, and the consequences, lying within a narrower field of vision, are more evident and affecting. An injurious system, the connivance at which we scarcely dare more than regret in the Cabinet or Senate of an Empire, may justify an earnest reprobation in the management of private Estates: provided always, that the System only be denounced, and the pleadings confined to the Court of Conscience. For from this court only can the redress be awarded. All Reform or Innovation, not won from the free Agent by the presentation of juster Views and nobler Interests, and that does not leave the merit of having effected it sacred to the individual proprietor, it were folly to propose, and worse than folly to attempt. Madmen only would dream of digging or blowing up the foundation of a House in order to employ the materials in repairing the walls. Nothing more dare be asked of the State, no other duty is imposed on it, than to withhold or retract all extrinsic and artificial aids to an injurious system; or at the utmost to invalidate in extreme cases such claims as have arisen indirectly from the letter or unforeseen operations of particular Statutes: claims that instead of being contained in the Rights of its proprietary Trustees are incroachments on its own Rights, and a destructive Trespass on a part of its own inalienable and untransferable Property—I mean the health, strength, honesty, and filial love of its children.

It would border on an affront to the understandings of our Landed Interest, were I to explain in detail what the plan and conduct would be of a gentleman;* if, as the result of his own free conviction the *marketable* produce of his Estates were made a subordinate consideration to the living and moral growth that is to remain on the land. I mean a healthful, callous-handed but high-and-warm-hearted Tenantry, twice the number of the present landless, parish-paid Laborers, and ready to march off at the first call of their country with a SON OF THE HOUSE at their head, because under no apprehension of being (forgive the lowness of the expression) *marched off* at the whisper of a Land-taster! If the admitted rule, the paramount *Self*-commandment, were comprized in

* Or, (to put the question more justly as well as more candidly) of the Land-owners collectively—for who is not aware of the facilities that accompany a conformity with the general practice, or of the numerous hindrances that retard, and the final imperfection that commonly awaits a deviation from it? On the distinction mentioned, p. 216, between Things and Persons, all law human and divine is grounded. It consists in this: that the former may be *used*, as *mere* means; but the latter *dare* not be employed as the means to an end without directly or indirectly sharing in that end.
See FRIEND, AMERICAN EDITION.

the fixed resolve—I will improve my *Estate* to the utmost; and my *rent-roll* I will raise as much as, but no more than, is compatible with the three great ends (before enumerated) which being those of my country must be mine inclusively! This, I repeat, it would be more than superfluous to particularize. It is a problem, the solution of which may be safely entrusted to the common sense of every one who has the hardihood to ask himself the question. But how encouraging even the approximations to such a system, of what fair promise the few fragmentary samples are, may be seen in the Report of the Board of Agriculture for 1816, p. 11, from the Earl of Winchelsea's communication, in every paragraph of which Wisdom seems to address us in behalf of Goodness.

But the plan of my argument requires the reverse of this picture. I am to ask what the results would be, on the supposition, that Agriculture is carried on in the spirit of Trade; and if the necessary answer coincide with the known general practice, to shew the connection of the consequences with the present state of distress and uneasiness. In Trade, from its most innocent form to the abomination of the

African commerce nominally abolished after a hard-fought battle of twenty years, no distinction is or can be acknowledged between Things and Persons. If the latter are part of the concern, they come under the denomination of the former. Two objects only can be proposed in the management of an Estate, considered as a *Stock* in Trade—first, that the Returns should be the largest, quickest, and securest possible; and secondly, with the least out-goings in the providing, over-looking, and collecting the same —whether it be expenditure of money paid for other mens' time and attention, or of the tradesman's own, which are to him *money's worth*, makes no difference in the argument. Am I disposing of a bale of goods? The man whom I most love and esteem must yield to the stranger that outbids him; or if it be sold on credit, the highest price, with equal security, must have the preference. I may fill up the deficiency of my friend's offer by a private gift, or loan; but as a tradesman, I am bound to regard honesty and established character themselves, as *things*, as *securities*, for which the known unprincipled dealer may offer an unexceptionable substitute. Add to this, that the security being equal, I shall prefer, even at a considerable abatement of price, the man who will take a thousand chests or bales at once, to twenty who can pledge themselves only for fifty each. For I do not seek trouble for its own sake; but among other advantages I seek wealth for the sake of freeing myself more and more from the necessity of taking trouble in order to attain it. The personal worth of those, whom I benefit in the course of the Process, or whether the persons are really benefited or no, is no concern of mine. The Market and the Shop are open to all. To introduce any other principle in Trade, but that of obtaining the highest price with adequate security for Articles fairly described, would be tantamount to the position, that Trade ought not to exist. If this be admitted, then what as a Tradesman I cannot do, it cannot be my Duty, as a Tradesman, to attempt: and the only remaining question in reason or morality is—what are the proper objects of Trade. If my Estate be such, my plan must be to make the most of it, as I would of any other mode of Capital. As my Rents will ultimately depend on the quantity and value of the Produce raised and brought into the best market from my Land, I will entrust the latter to those who bidding the most have the largest Capital to employ on it: and this I cannot effect but by dividing it into the fewest Tenures, as none but extensive Farms will be an object to men of extensive capital and enterprizing minds. I must prefer this system likewise for my own ease and security. The Farmer is of course actuated by the same motives, as the Landlord: and, provided they are both faithful to their engagements, the objects of both will be: 1. the utmost Produce that can be raised without injuring the estate; 2. with the least possible consumption of the Produce on the Estate itself; 3. at the lowest wages; and 4. with the substitution of machinery for human labor where ever the former will cost less and do the same work. What are the modest remedies proposed by the majority of correspondents in the last Report of the Board of Agriculture? Let measures be taken, that rents, taxes, and wages be lowered, and the Markets raised! A great calamity has befallen us, from importation, the lessened purchases of Government, and "*the evil of a superabundant Harvest*"—of which we deem ourselves the more entitled to complain, because "*we had been long making* 112 *shillings per quarter of our Corn,*" and of all other articles in proportion. As the best remedies for this calamity, we propose that we should pay less to our Landlords, less to our Laborers, nothing to our Clergyman, and either nothing or very little to the maintenance of the Government and of the Poor; but that we should sell at our former prices to the Consumer!—In almost every page we find deprecations of the Poor Laws: and I hold it impossible to exaggerate their pernicious tendency and consequences. But let it not be forgotten, that in agricultural districts three-forths of the Poors' Rates are paid to healthy, robust, and (O sorrow and shame!) *industrious, hard-working* Paupers in lieu of Wages —(for men cannot at once work and starve:) and therefore if there are twenty House-keepers in the Parish, who are not holders of Land, their contributions are so much Bounty Money to the latter. But the Poor Laws form a subject, which I should not undertake without trembling, had I the space of a whole volume to allot to it. Suffice, that this enormous mischief is *undeniably* the offspring of the Commercial System. In the only plausible Work, that I have seen, in favor of our Poor Laws on the present plan, the Defence is grounded: first, on the expediency of having Labor cheap, and Estates let out in the fewest possible portions—in other words, of large Farms and low Wages—each as indispensable to the other, and both conjointly as the only means of drawing Capital to the Land, by which alone the largest Surplus is attainable for the *State:* that is, for the Market, or in order that the smallest possible proportion of the largest possible Produce may be consumed by the Raisers and their families! Secondly, on the impossibility of supplying, as we have supplied, all the countries of the civilized World (India perhaps and China excepted) and of underselling them even in their own markets, if our *working* Manufactures were not secured by the State against the worst consequences of those failures, stagnations, and transfers, to which the different branches of Trade are exposed, in a greater or less degree, beyond all human prevention; or if the *Master* Manufacturers were compelled to give previous security for the maintenance of those whom they had, by the known Law of human Increase, virtually called into existence.

Let me not be misunderstood. I do not myeslf admit this impossibility. I have already denied, and I now repeat the denial, that these are *necessary* consequences of our extended Commerce. On the contrary, I feel assured that the Spirit of Commerce is itself capable of being at once counteracted and enlightened by the Spirit of the State, to the advantage of both. But I *do* assert, that they are necessary consequences of the Commercial Spirit un-counteracted and *un*-enlightened, wherever Trade has been carried to so vast an extent as it has in England. I assert too, historically and as matter of fact, that they *have been the* consequence of our commercial system. The laws of Lycurgus, like those of the inspired Hebrew Legislator, were anticommercial: those of Solon and Numa were at least uncommercial. Now I ask myself, what the impression would have been on the Senate of the Roman or of the Athenian Republic, if the following proposal had been made to them and introduced by the following preamble. "Conscript Fathers, (or Senators of Athens!) it is well known to you, that circumstances being the same and the time allowed proportional, the human animal may be made to multiply as easily, and at as small an expence, as your sheep or swine: which is meant, perhaps, in the fiction of our philosophers, that Souls are out of all proportion more numerous than the Bodies, in which they can subsist and be manifested. It is likewise known to you, Fathers! that though in various States various checks have been ordained to prevent this increase of births from becoming such as should frustrate or greatly endanger the ends for which freemen are born; yet the most efficient limit must be sought for in the moral and intellectual prerogatives of men, in their foresight, in their habituation to the comforts and decencies of society, in the pride of independence; but above all in THE HOPE that enables men to withstand the tyranny of the present impulse, and in their expectation of honor or discredit from the rank, character, and condition of their children. Now there are proposed to us the speedy means of at once increasing the number of the rich, the wealth of those that are already such, and the revenues of the State: and the latter, Fathers!

to so vast an amount, that we shall be able to pay not only our own soldiers but those of the monarchs whom we may thus induce to become our Allies. But for this it will be requisite and indispensable that all men of enterprize and sufficiency among us should be permitted, without restraint, to encourage, and virtually to occasion, the birth of many myriads of free citizens, who from their childhood are to be amassed in clusters and employed as parts of a mighty system of machinery. While all things prove answerable to the schemes and wishes of these enterprisers, the Citizens thus raised and thus employed by them will find an ample maintenance, except in such instances where the individual may have rendered himself useless by the effects of his own vices. It dare not, however, be disguised from you, that the nature of the employments and the circumstances to which these citizens will be exposed, will often greatly tend to render them intemperate, diseased, and restless. Nor has it been yet made a part of the proposal, that the employers should be under any bond to counteract such injurious circumstances by education, discipline, or other efficient regulations. Still less may it be withheld from your knowledge, O Fathers of the State, that should events hereafter prove hostile to all or to any branch of these speculations, to many or to any one of the number that shall have devoted their wealth to the realization of the same—and the light, in which alone they can thrive, is confessedly subject to partial and even to total eclipses, which there are no means of precisely foretelling! the guardian planets, to whose conjunction their success is fatally linked, will at uncertain periods, for a longer or shorter time, act in malignant oppositions!—Then, Fathers, the Principals are to shift for themselves, and leave the disposal of the calamitous, and therefore too probably turbulent, multitude, now unemployed and useless, to the mercy of the community, and the solicitude of the State: to expose to famine, violence, and the vengeance of the Laws!"

If, on the maxims of ancient prudence, on the one hand not enlightened, on the other not misled by the principles of Trade, the immediate answer would have been:—"We should deem it danger and detriment, were we to permit so indefinite and improvident increase even of our Slaves and Helots: in the case of free Citizens, our countrymen, who are to swear to the same laws, and worship at the same altars, it were profanation! May the Gods avert the Omen!"—If this, I say, would have been their rescript, it may be safely concluded, that the connivance at the same scheme, much more that the direct encouragement of it, must be attributed to that spirit which the ancients did not recognize, namely, the Spirit of Commerce.

But we have shewn, that the same system has gradually taken possession of our agriculture. What have been the results? For him who is either unable or unwilling to deduce the whole truth from the portion of it revealed in the following extract from Lord Winchelsea's Report, whatever I could have added would have been equally in vain. His Lordship speaking of the causes which oppose all attempts to better the Laborers condition, mentions, as one great cause, the dislike the generality of Farmers have to seeing the Laborers rent any land. Perhaps, (he continues) "one of the reasons for their disliking this is, that the land, if not occupied by the laborers, would fall to their own share; and another I am afraid is, that they rather wish to have the laborers more dependant upon them; for which reasons they are always desirous of hiring the house and land occupied by a laborer, under pretence, that by that means the landlord will be secure of his rent, and that they will keep the house in repair. This the agents of estates are too apt to give into, as they find it much less trouble to meet six than sixty tenants at a rent-day, and by this means avoid the being sometimes obliged to hear the wants and complaints of the poor. All parties therefore join in pursuading the landlord, who it is natural to suppose (unless he has time and inclination to investigate the matter very closely) will agree to this their plan, from the manner in which it comes recommended to him: and it is in this manner that the laborers have been dispossessed of their cow-pastures in various parts of the midland counties. The moment the farmer obtains his wish, he takes every particle of the land to himself, and re-lets the house to the laborer, who by this means is rendered miserable; the Poor Rate increased; the value of the Estate to the Landowner diminished; and the house suffered to go to decay: which once fallen the tenant will never rebuild, but the landlord must, at a considerable expence. Whoever travels through the midland counties, and will take the trouble of enquiring, will generally receive for an answer, that formerly there were a great many cottagers who kept cows, but that the land is now thrown to the farmers; and if he enquires still farther, he will find that in those parishes the poors' rates have increased in an amazing degree, more than according to the average rise throughout England."—In confirmation of his Lordship's statement I find in the Agricultural Reports, that the county, in which I read of nothing but farms of 1000, 1500, 2000, and 2500 acres, is likewise that in which the poor rates are most numerous, the distresses of the poor most grievous, and the prevalence of revolutionary principles the most alarming. But if we consider the subject on the largest scale and nationally, the consequences are, that the most important rounds in the social ladder are broken, and the Hope, which above all other things distinguishes the free man from the slave, is extinguished. The peasantry therefore are eager to have their children add as early as possible to their wretched pittances, by letting them out to manufactories; while the youths take every opportunity of escaping to towns and cities. And if I were questioned, as to my opinion respecting the ultimate cause of our liability to distresses like the present, the cause of what has been called a vicious (i. e. excessive) population with all the furies that follow in its train—in short, of the state of things so remote from the simplicity of nature that we have almost deprived Heaven itself of the power of blessing us; a state in which, without absurdity, a superabundant Harvest can be complained of as an evil, and the recurrence of the same a ruinous calamity—I should not hesitate to answer—*the vast and disproportionate number of men who are to be fed from the produce of the fields, on which they do not labor.*

What then is the remedy? Who the physicians? The reply may be anticipated. An evil, which has come on gradually, and in the growth of which all men have more or less conspired, cannot be removed otherwise than gradually, and by the joint efforts of all. If we are a christian nation, we must learn to act nationally as well as individually, as Christians.

We must remove half-truths, the most dangerous of errors (as those of the poor visionaries called SPENCEANS) by the whole Truth. The Government is employed already in retrenchments; but he who expects immediate relief from these, or who does not even know that if they do any thing at all, they must for the time tend to aggravate the distress, cannot have studied the operation of public expenditure.

I am persuaded that more good would be done, not only ultimate and permanent, but immediate, good, by the abolition of the Lotteries accompanied with a public and parliamentary declaration of the moral and religious grounds that had determined the Legislature to this act; of their humble confidence in the blessing of God on the measure; and of their hopes that this sacrifice to principle, as being more exemplary from the present pressure on the Revenue of the State, would be the more effective in restoring confidence between man and man—I am deeply convinced, that more sterling and visible benefits would be derived from this one solemn proof and pledge of moral fortitude and national faith, than from retrenchments to a tenfold greater amount. Still more, if our

Legislators should pledge themselves at the same time, that they would hereafter take council for the gradual removal or counteraction of all similar encouragements and temptations to Vice and Folly, that had alas! been tolerated hitherto, as the easiest way of supplying the exchequer. And truly, the financial motives would be strong indeed, if the Revenue Laws in question were but half as productive of money to the State as they are of guilt and wretchedness to the people.

Our manufacturers must consent to regulations; our gentry must concern themselves in the *education* as well as in the *instruction* of their natural clients and dependents, must regard their estates as secured indeed from all human interference by every principle of law, and policy, but yet as offices of trust, with duties to be performed, in the sight of God and their Country. Let us become a better people, and the reform of all the public (real or supposed) grievances, which we use as pegs whereon to hang our own errors and defects, will follow of itself. In short, let every man measure his efforts by his power and his sphere of action, and do all he can do! Let him contribute money where he cannot act personally; *but let him act personally and in detail* wherever it is practicable. Let us palliate where we cannot cure, comfort where we cannot relieve; and for the rest rely upon the promise of the King of Kings by the mouth of his Prophet, "BLESSED ARE YE THAT SOW BESIDE ALL WATERS."

LaVergne, TN USA
29 November 2010
206609LV00003BA/22/P